Conservatories and patios

 AREND JAN VAN DER HORST

INTRODUCTION BY RICHARD ROSENFELD

REBO
PRODUCTIONS

© 1995 Zuid Boekprodukties, Lisse
© 1997 Published by Rebo Productions Ltd
Text: *Arend Jan van der Horst*
Cover design: *Ton Wienbelt, The Netherlands*
Picture editing: *Marieke Uiterwijk*
Production: *TextCase, The Netherlands*
Translation: *Mary Boorman for First Edition Translations Ltd, Great Britain*
Typesetting: *Fairfield Systems for First Edition Translations Ltd, Great Britain*

ISBN 1 901094 35 9

Contents

INTRODUCTION

You can always spot the true gardener, the one with real ambition, by his line-up of conservatory plants. They're a way of looking inside his head. At his multi-coloured, jungly dreams. Because in conservatories you can grow what you want. *Kohleria* and *Caladium*, *Lotus* and *Tweedia*, the wonderful, poisonous *Datura* (once a favourite form of suicide in India), even Meditteranean *Bougainvilleas*.

Conservatories (or posh greenhouses without the mud) are quite a recent invention. It all began when John Evelyn started referring to a *greene house* in the 1660s. By which he meant a place where tender plants might just about survive in winter, provided the outside temperatures weren't too savage, and the fires or stoves did not go out. Evelyn, incidentally, could be a bit of a devil. He once made inquiries about getting a *"subtil and industrious person [to] smuggle a seed or two from the plantations . . . as that countrie man of ours, who some years since brought home the first heads of saffron out of Greece (whence it was death to transport) in the hollow head or top of his pilgrim staff."* Then, as now, illegal seed collecting can land you in jail.

It is maddeningly ironic that while the great plant hunters were running round the world from the 16th century, chasing fruits and plants and exotica, living in massive cantankerous ships, and risking their lives (like a chap called David Nelson, the fresh-faced young gardener on the *HMS Bounty*, who saw his collection of 1,005 breadfruit and rattah trees hurled into the sea by mutineers), they did not always know how to care for them. They did not have books like this.

Evelyn's best piece of advice was to rub honey over the plant. Others used ox bladders as glorified plant pots; in went the rootball with the stem sticking out of the neck. In the mid 18th century Carl Linnaeus came up with the idea of packing seed in corked bottles of sand, and later on collectors started putting seed in boxes of beeswax. No one knows exactly how the industrious Rev. John Banister packed his fabulous collection of N. American plants back to Henry Compton's magical Brompton Park nursery in Fulham in the late 17th century that

covered 100 acres, and stocked 40,000 plants, but clearly some collectors were getting it right. And after the invention of the Wardian case (a sealed glass case available to collectors from the 1830s), success rates really rocketed.

The end result is that today you can more or less grow what you want. Rampant climbing flowerers, grapes, and scented plants, and best of all you can give what are normally thought of as small pot plants a free run in the conservatory border, and watch them sprint up a wall. Plants like *Heliotropium* and *Pelargoniums* can actually grow 2m (6ft), provided they are carefully tied in.

Most conservatory plants, except the really precious, enjoy plenty of fresh air over summer. Placing them outside on the patio for a few weeks perks them up, and gives you a chance to open the conservatory, stopping the build-up of swarming pests. The two go hand-in-hand. And it's such a simple job, when building on a conservatory, to create a few square yards of flat stone where you can stand the plants in the open. It also toughens them up. The inside heating is usually infallible, but there's always one night in winter, when the electricity suddenly cuts. Don't over-pamper your plants. It's not always a good idea!

Richard Rosenfeld, East Sussex, 1997.

The warmth of brick walls

I well remember a visit I once made to some enthusiastic gardeners in the Netherlands, where the degeneration of an old part of the town has been halted by sensitive action.

The town council was confronted with old houses almost all of which had a large or small garden area at the back. A decision was taken to create access to the gardens via a lane behind them. This sometimes meant the loss of a section of the garden. The existing boundaries of all the gardens had to go, and the brilliant plan was put forward to surround each garden with a wall. That was a very expensive operation and one which the average new owner of an old property could not have afforded. It was a good investment, because with the addition of walls even the smallest area became an attractive outdoor room.

I sat with my host in a patio-type garden about 4m (13ft) square. The brick walls made it a very pleasant situation and there was the feeling that no neighbour or passer-by could disturb the cosy atmosphere. It was obvious just how important the walls were to that tiny garden. A hedge or a screen of shrubs would never have given such a feeling of security and privacy. The walls round this garden were high enough to prevent people looking over, so they must have been about 2m (6ft) high.

I remember that it was paved with natural stone cobbles of grey granite. A grapevine grew against the wall, there were pots with annuals, and there was space for a round table and easy chairs where you could sit in comfort until far into the night.

Bricks hold warmth, so in old country houses the vegetable garden was always surrounded by brick walls, which had espalier fruit trees on the south-facing side. Here there is an ornamental vine, Vitis coignetiae, *which has pretty dark purple colouring in the autumn.*

Plaster a drab stone outhouse and add some Spanish or Tuscan details such as hanging geraniums, small pillars and a sundial on the wall. In Tuscany the walls would be ochre or rust coloured, in Spain they are white.

The longing for some sort of enclosure is pretty well universal, everyone is looking for a place outside where they can be undisturbed. Or so I thought until I met several garden lovers who found such places claustrophobic and preferred to sit in an open meadow. But they are in a minority.

When I was designing a garden for a bungalow that stood on the edge of a town it occurred to me that there can be variations on small enclosed spaces. On one side lay fields and canals as far as the eye could see. And the garden needed a wall round it because of the wind there. It happened that three sides were protected by the walls of the bungalow and a wall only had to be built on the south west, which was the direction of the prevailing wind. After some thought, I designed a wall with a sliding wooden panel in it which could be opened if the wind permitted. I had a large wooden terrace built in front of the sliding section, to which I added further square terraces, a large pool, and then decorated with several attractive roses and perennials.

So if the weather permitted the patio could be opened out, and in windy weather it became a sheltered, enclosed garden.

At Powis Castle, Herefordshire, on the border between England and Wales, there is an interesting garden. Apart from the lovely borders, statues, greenhouses, and parterres there are also warm brick walls with seats in pastel colours. The cistern is made of lead.

A garden in Drenthe, in the Netherlands

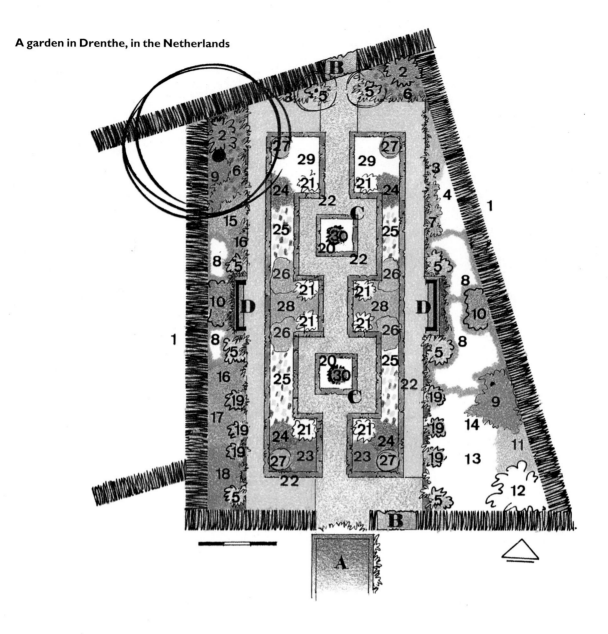

A bakehouse on the centuries-old farm in
  Drenthe

B gateways through beech hedges

C *Juniperus communis*, juniper, forms
  central, evergreen pillars

D seats

1 hedge of *Fagus sylvaticus*

2 *Levisticum officinale*, lovage

3 *Tanacetum vulgare*, tansy

4 *Mentha rotundifolia*, 'Variegata',
  apple mint

5 *Artemisia absinthium*, wormwood

6 *Fragaria vesca*, wild strawberry

7 *Thymus vulgaris*, common thyme

8 *Mentha piperata*, peppermint

9 *Salvia sclarea*, clary

10 *Valeriana officinalis*, valerian

11 *Agastache foeniculum*, mexican
  hyssop

12 *Angelica archangelica*, angelica

13 *Armoracia rusticana*, horseradish

14 *Myrrhis odorata*, sweet cicely

15 *Coriandrum sativum*, coriander

16 *Sanguisorba minor*, salad burnet

17 *Satureja montana*, winter savory

18 *Origanum vulgare*, marjoram

19 *Allium schoenoprasum*, chives

20 *Anthemis nobilis*, camomile

21 *Artemisia abrotanum*, southernwood

22 low hedges of various herbs e.g.
  Lavendula, Teucrium, Santolina,
  Nepeta, Origanum

23 *Ocimum basilicum*, basil

24 *Aconitum napellus*, monkshood

25 *Viola tricolor*, heartsease

26 *Anchusa officianalis*, borage

27 *Ruta graveolens*, rue

28 *Teucrium chamaedrys*, wall
  germander

29 *Asperula odorata*, woodruff

30 *Juniperus communis*, juniper

Wood for solid or open fences

If you walk into a more or less forgotten little garden in an old town you often see a greenish, mouldy fence that has almost collapsed from neglect.

Yet there are positive discoveries to be made after the first negative impressions of a garden and fence like that. If the owner wants a new design there is usually an old elderberry somewhere, or a tall *Aucuba* or a grotesquely shaped *Rhododendron*, which can form part of it. The fence may seem to have practically collapsed but with a few new posts even a fence like that will often last for years longer, keeping the lovely colours which result from years of weathering.

I recall the lovely blue-green tints of fences and garden sheds which were once stained green. In many cases people clear everything away that is old in the desire to tidy up. They don't look with sympathetic eyes and imagine a pale pink or violet *Clematis* against an old fence which would make a positive feature of it. There is often a reason for this urge to change things: people want "privacy" straight away and they choose the easiest option, solid fencing.

Old-fashioned horizontal planking

In the past the use of hardwood was unknown in gardens and timber was preserved rather crudely with creosote. Even tar was used. These substances are harmful to the plants nearby. In warm weather oil seeps out which scorches the plants. So other solutions were sought. Now there are all kinds of stain, external quality of course, which will not harm plants growing close to the fence. There are also treated planks and posts which are greenish in colour. These will later turn grey, but the colour will remain pale. And of course

Netting can be fixed to fences to provide support for sweet peas, Lathyrus. Cutting the flowers regularly ensures blooms until the cold weather comes.

An ideal support for climbing and twining plants can be made by fixing trellis to the wooden fence. This is very attractive.

nowadays there is hardwood, but more of that later. The most common method of fixing the planks upright is to attach them to concrete posts sunk in the ground. This is a fairly crude method, but it is fine if the posts are hidden. Yet many people have something against concrete so wooden posts are often chosen for the uprights. Pressure-treated posts have a guaranteed life of fifteen years, which is reasonable, and they are therefore the most popular kind. Besides, they are cheap and easy to work with.

If the planks are fixed horizontally and if furthermore they are tongued and grooved so that they fit tightly together, there is a minimal chance of rot caused by penetration of damp. With very high-quality fences there is a lead or zinc rim round the lowest plank to protect against damp and rot.

You can sometimes come across coloured fences. With an old house it can be attractive to paint the horizontal planks green and the groove between the tongued and grooved planks white. This does not in general go well with new building. But perhaps you are going to ignore that and turn the rather dull fence of your new house into a rustic division with dark green planks separated by white stripes.

It can be exciting and unexpected and could perhaps form the boundary of a pleasant rural garden.

Anyone who is fond of peaceful surroundings and sees the fence as just a necessary evil can conceal the boundary in no time at all with

This wooden fencing has been stained brown, giving a warm background for colourful perennials.

a profusion of climbing plants. But do not make the mistake of planting a Russian vine against your fence. If ever there was an uncontrollable plant, it is the Russian vine, which is a member of the *Polygonum* family. Roses, grapevines, wisteria, clematis, honeysuckle, kiwi, the possibilities are endless. Try to reflect the colours of plants further away in the garden in the flowers or foliage of the climbers and then success will be assured.

Vertical planking

I usually have the planks running vertically on the fences that I design – that is, the grooves run up and down. The advantage is that the line then matches the vertical lines of trees, individuals that always grow upwards and thus show ascending form and rhythm. Besides, that makes a wooden wall appear shorter and it fits in with the ascending pattern of twigs and branches.

An open-work wooden fence

For many years my section of the roof garden in my town house was divided from my neighbours' by woven fencing. This was made of treated pine that soon became grey. The narrow planks were bent or woven round uprights, which gave a pattern of horizontal lines. I found it a bit of a nuisance at first that the horizontal gaps meant that the neighbours and I could peer at each other.

This problem was soon solved, however, with a lot of pots of ivy and honeysuckle. I would have been satisfied with it for many more

This system is known as tongue-and-groove. A narrow ridge on the upper edge of the plank (the tongue) fits into a narrow groove on the lower edge of the plank above it. Here is an imaginative garden based on roof tiles on a ledge, with all kinds of Sedum *and* Sempervivum *which can grow without soil.*

11

years but then I got neighbours who were so obtrusive that I decided to put up a closed fence of white-painted pine planking.

This shows the dilemma of open trellis-work; it is fine if you want to some extent to see what it conceals, such as the vegetable garden or a public open space. If it is a question of a car park or a busy road, or the fence directly borders the neighbours' terrace, then a great many climbing plants must be used if you want to make trellis-work sufficiently "closed".

So open-work fencing is very useful if the surroundings are peaceful. In a patio garden I designed for a dentist in Haarlem open trellis was used. It is not a large garden, but it gives a very good idea of the possibilities.

In old gardening books there are illustrations of different ways of training fruit trees. There is a strong pattern here where the vertical planking contrasts with the diagonals of the cordon pear trees.

Open trellis used as a boundary

To avoid a feeling of claustrophobia in the smaller garden or court-yard area open wooden screens can be used, staggered along the boundaries.

I designed wooden screens which stood a little way from the boundary and planted bamboo behind them. The bamboo is now growing through the screens, which are partly covered by honeysuckle. So there is a unity between wood and planting. Three-quarters of the way down the garden a screen has been set crosswise, so that it makes an angle. There too the laths are vertical and open. What lies behind is not totally visible, depth and surprise have been created. A

Japanese theme was chosen for the design by using white gravel, a pool on two levels, and Japanese-style planting. So as well as the bamboos there are several ornamental pines which have blue-green needles. They are called *Pinus parviflora*, Japanese white pine, and they grow superbly without any attention. A very airy, exciting garden has developed with the wooden screens, which have also been used to keep out unwelcome visitors. Pruning is essential here to keep the bamboos under control, otherwise this kind of garden would soon become overgrown and lose its transparent character.

If you want to have a screen in summer that is open in the winter you will enjoy having a rose hedge. Put up a trellis, paint it dark green, and train the roses up it.

The twining climber Ipomoea, *morning glory, winds its way to the top of the fence in one summer and flowers freely.*

Paving for paths and terraces

There are materials that are nice to use in any garden. Whether a house is old or modern there are "evergreens" that can safely be chosen.

First of all there are bricks or pavers. These can be obtained in various colours. They reflect the colour of the clay used. Bricks from the Weald in south-east England are brown or red. Round the Thames estuary the chalky clays bake to bright yellow or even a dark purple, producing the famous London "stocks". The Gault clays of East Anglia give yellow bricks, the so-called "white" bricks.

The warm red shades are the most appropriate for the garden, certainly for a patio where people are sitting looking at them all day. The varied colours of the rectangular bricks which differ slightly in colour are attractive and never boring. Clay bricks keep their colour too and mellow over the years instead of becoming uglier, which is what happens with a lot of concrete blocks.

There are a number of specialist bricks, which can be prohibitively expensive for some gardeners. Those who have the money and are willing to spend the time needed to track them down can have splendid terraces paved with bricks of various shapes and sizes.

Traditionally paths and terraces are paved with bricks in a herringbone pattern. Many types of brick are suitable and they fit closely. Stretcher bond is also a good choice, provided a firm edge is put in.

Concrete pavers will, however, suit more pockets because they are much cheaper than bricks. Besides, they are a regular shape and so there is less problem with weeds in the gaps than when using bricks. They come in many colours, but you must be sure to ask for extra

A sandpit beside an old path made of setts. These give an old-fashioned air to the garden, adding substance to the smallest path. The various colours are a bonus.

information about the colour. It needs to be all the way through otherwise after several years of sun and rain the colour will have faded. You should be able to obtain concrete blocks which have been put through a mill so that the edges and corners have been smoothed off to make them look older. When they are being laid grooves can be left so that mosses, small thyme plants, or seeds of lady's mantle can become established among the stones. A more mellow effect is possible with these blocks than with the standard concrete blocks that have not been milled. I would make a plea for using a combination of old bricks and new concrete blocks if money is limited. Remember too that making some investigations among gardeners, garden centres and dealers in old building materials could result in finding attractive materials at easily affordable prices.

Bricks absorb moisture. It could be better to choose a lighter paving material than setts if the area where a terrace is to be laid is damp and gets little light. Here light ornaments and furniture have been chosen.

Slabs Many gardeners think of slabs as concrete slabs, and rightly so because the majority of gardens have that kind. Anyone who wants a more original effect will have to look for an alternative. But there is nothing against the use of brownish, dark grey, or yellowish-red slabs and they will undoubtedly continue to be widely used. Concrete slabs have a bad name because people think of the monotonous grey of paving slabs. And yet even paving slabs are nice when combined with bricks, gravel, or perhaps with small pebbles. Make

15

Concrete slabs with a layer of pebbles have become fashionable where in the past natural stone would have been chosen. Provided the pebbles are not too big or too white they make an acceptable paving for paths. For terraces I would advise a combination with cobbles or bricks or choose one of each.

squares of slabs and put the other materials round them to make simple, interesting paths and terraces.

In the spring and summer these paths and terraces will be less noticeable because of all the flowering plants on and alongside them, but in autumn and winter a variety of paving gives a pleasing effect.

Personally I like three kinds of concrete slabs. To begin with, I approve of 50 x 50cm (20 x 20in) slabs because these create space. They can be laid like stepping stones in paths with gravel or plants in between, or in a terrace with a 20cm (8in) wide border of brick, pebbles or gravel round every four tiles. This gives variety, especially when there is a plant in a container here and there. Choose some-thing with large leaves such as *Bergenia, Darmera (Peltiphyllum)* or *Ligularia* as a major element.

The second type of slab that I find attractive is the 40 x 60cm (16 x 24in) size. These are laid widthways. This creates an effect of breadth for paths and terraces. They can also be laid with the edges staggered so that little corners are created for smaller low-growing plants.

My third choice of concrete slabs is the dark grey or almost black type because these give a neutral depth to the garden. When they are used it seems as if the paving fades away and all the attention is focused on the plants, walls, and ornaments.

Quarry tiles are not usually frost-proof so in our climate we are fortunate to have conservatories, dining rooms, and kitchens where we can use them and enjoy their warm colour.

Concrete setts   You can achieve attractive paving by using concrete setts, which mostly come in the size 10 x 10cm (4 x 4in). They are often light or dark grey.

There are also 15 x 15cm (6 x 6in) concrete setts. These can often be obtained in various colour combinations, which vary from brownish yellow and reddish purple to light yellow.

Natural stone for tiles and cobbles   In the south of the Netherlands and in Belgium, Germany, France and Britain you can often see natural stone from quarries used as paving. The well-known cut stones, sometimes called setts, are mainly of granite or basalt. Granite has light flecks, basalt is the same colour all over. The colours vary, especially in granite.

As the light fades so the colours fade, but if they are well chosen there are still subtle colour combinations.

A patio garden with pebbles   A good example of the use of this material is in the Maastricht garden in the photograph on this page, in which attractive light-coloured granite setts have been used.

As an architect and garden designer you learn to work with angles and straight lines. Is that why so many designs consist of straight lines? They are obviously very popular with those two groups of people.

It was quite a breakthrough for me to discover a garden designer in Brazil who thought in terms of curved, natural lines which flow. His name is Roberto Burle Marx and the book in which I made the

At this farmhouse gravel has been used. Perennials in delicate shades combine with it effectively.

discovery is a German publication called *The Tropical Gardens of Roberto Burle Marx*.

Following in his footsteps, I am still designing gardens with flowing lines, but to be fair I must admit that it is by no means always possible in the Netherlands, with the straight lines of dykes, canals, as well as roads.

In a completely walled patio garden in Maastricht all the lines were almost out of true or at an angle, so that there was no real reason to start working with artificial, regular shapes.

I designed a courtyard which is divided with tall yew hedges, so that there is an outer courtyard and a hidden inner courtyard.

The yew hedges and paths curve round in flowing lines which are very effective because they are unfamiliar and unexpected. Those who come here find them surprising.

And yet ... there is a long tradition of designing parks and very large gardens in the so-called landscape style in which curved lines were used.

The pebbles in this garden have been laid at random, more or less in a fan shape. The paved area therefore flows between the plants, becoming wider or narrower. My clients were against the idea of having the irregular pebbles for their sitting area by the house and chose instead the same tiles that were used indoors: dark grey natural stone. So unfortunately there was a division in the garden

Shells can be washed and then used on paths and open areas in the garden. They are also appropriate in coastal nature reserves.

Both these photographs were taken in the garden of the National Institute for War Records on the Herengracht in Amsterdam, where I designed a garden of classic simplicity. Right at the back there was a wall covered in ivy, a plant which makes a perfect camouflage for ugly walls, chain link, or not very successful trellis-work. On the pedestal in the centre there is a bronze faun. Shells were used on the paths round the knot garden.

18

between the terrace and the pebbles. If the pebbles had gone right up to the back of the house there would have been an effect of greater depth and the garden would have looked bigger.

The planting in this garden   The dividing hedges are of *Taxus baccata*, which remains dark green throughout the winter.

The view from the house is along the brick wall on the right-hand side. Against the sunny wall a herbaceous border was planted in deep pinks, with some roses in it. On the shady side, to the left, were ground cover and plants with large leaves in shades of yellow, while a circular pool became the central point in the outer court-yard. Ornamental apples have been planted for their blossom and red fruit, forming an attractive feature.

To disguise the high wall on the left some round-headed acacias have been planted and a *Catalpa bignonioides*, Indian bean tree. Where the space is divided I had an arbour built for the children to swing and play house; one of the daughters had her own little gar-den there too.

At the very far end of the garden there is a fruit border with grapevines against the wall, berries, rhubarb and wild strawberries. There are also some herbs.

On the left at the back, in a hidden courtyard, round beds have been planted with standard roses. I also had a stout hardwood post set up

here. On the top there is a hook to which one end of a hammock can be attached. The other end can be fixed to a similar hook on the wall. To give the post a second function I planted wisteria against it. This has now grown into a beautiful flowering tree.

We also put here a seat that was given to the owners by a number of their friends when the garden was finished.

It is a wonderful place to sit, away from the telephone and the everyday pressures, which makes it possible to study in peace, to chat, or just be lazy.

There is no fencing in this garden. If there had been I would have followed the line of the chair backs and used vertical planks. In that way shapes can be related within a design.

The enormous fruit garden of this seventeenth-century house in England is surrounded by a high brick wall with fruit trees trained against it. The fruit museum of the National Trust is housed here. Here you can see Clematis montana.

For a town garden I once designed a range of possibilities which are shown below. It is important to know what the surrounding areas are used for. At the bottom there is the large kitchen/dining room which has tall windows overlooking the garden. To the left in a sort of identation there is the entrance to the living room. Also on the left, but higher up, there is a greenhouse that could be built round or could be kept as a romantic place for tender plants. The large circles are trees which are already there. On the right there is the very old, high and weathered town wall and above it is a barn/garage shown by a dark line. This is a true patio, fully enclosed, which makes a very good place to sit. Behind the conservatory-greenhouse shown above left is the blank wall of the historic house. The courtyard has brick paths and terraces.

A town garden

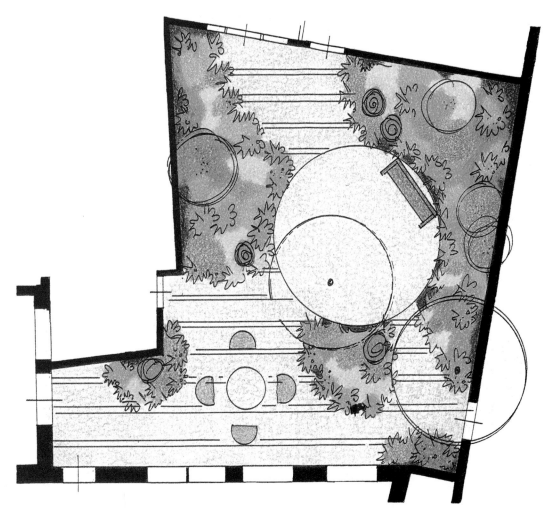

This design is simpler, with a lot of space for walking and sitting, a small cistern with a spout (to drown out the sounds from outside), and a large square bed with box edging in a shape that recalls the gardens in medieval monasteries and herb gardens.

A vertical element has been introduced into the garden by building a pergola over the sitting area and seat.

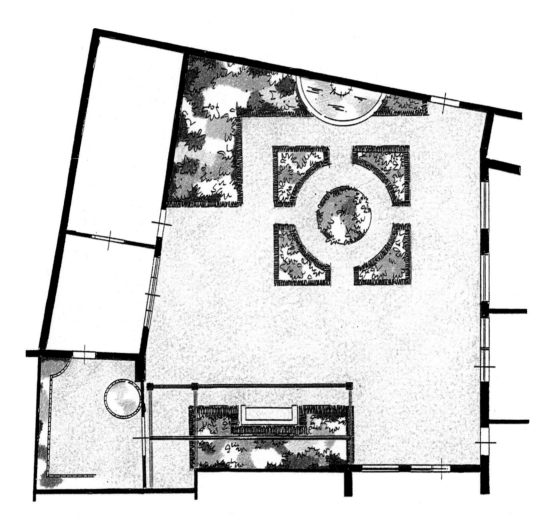

This variation is mid-way between the somewhat formal geometric design and the informality of the first design. It goes without saying that in a garden like this the planting is kept free and light-hearted to provide a contrast with the straight lines of the paths and the six austere blocks of box or yew. The chairs, modelled on French bistro chairs, add a lively touch to the garden.

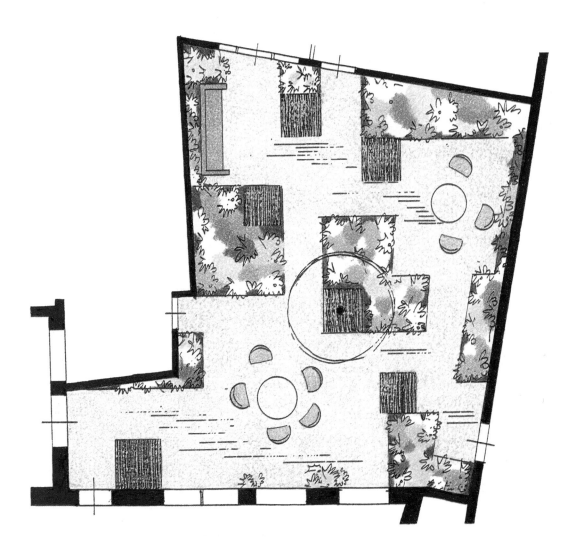

This design is a variation on a simple design with a lot of space for walking and sitting. Part of that space has been taken up by four extra box-edged beds. There is more green in the garden, which gives it more vitality.

This garden has been kept more "horizontal" than the second one – there are no vertical elements such as the pergola. The planting along the house walls consists of taller-growing plants such as small shrubs of upright growth form.

Wooden decking for paths and floors

Anybody who sails knows the feeling of excitement when walking on wooden jetties. I certainly find it thrilling. I am walking above the water, there is usually no handrail, and so there is a sense of suspense, of "mind you don't fall in".

This feeling has probably been an important source of inspiration for many people who want to introduce wood into the garden.

Wood and water go together and usually in a patio garden with a wooden deck there is also a pool – not that this is strictly necessary, because pebbles could be used instead of a pool, with a number of large bird baths that are filled regularly or several barrels planted with water plants. Not everyone is keen on water, because of the midges and the danger to children, so I shall discuss decks for both a "dry" and a "wet" garden.

The deck in a "dry" garden

On my many visits to Japanese temple gardens I have seen that water is certainly not always featured when there is a wooden terrace; there are beautiful gardens with and without it. The temples almost always have wooden floors, like the traditional houses. The floors are raised to keep the wood off the damp earth and to allow the wind to dry the underneath. Moss and gravel are often used as ground covering where there is a view, with maples, azaleas, bamboo, and some pruned conifers. Gravel and wood look lovely together, so this is a good combination for western gardens too.

Behind the idea of raising up the planks used to build up footpaths or terraces is a good reason and an age-old tradition: the wood rots more slowly if the underside is not in contact with the earth. Raising

Wooden decking can be made of hardwood that bleaches or of treated pine that can be stained, as you see here. You can also leave it grey-green and the colour will fade over time. Here the deck, which has been stained black, goes well with the silver-grey hardwood furniture.

25

them up gives a floating effect too, which is not the case when they are bedded on sand.

The Japanese attach a symbolic meaning to their gravel courtyard gardens but that is more difficult for westerners. Designers can get some inspiration from Japan nevertheless. Gravel often symbolizes water – a river, a lake, or the sea. It is raked into wave patterns. This is done with a coarse wooden rake, reminiscent of the old-fashioned hay rakes once used by farmers. People do not walk on the gravel because that would signify walking on water, which is impossible. There is no such problem of symbolism in using gravel round decks in the west. It is nice to give a watery "feel" to gravel by the choice of appropriate plants. This can be achieved by planting bamboo, tall ornamental grasses, and plants such as *Hosta*, *Ligularia*, and butterbur which have large leaves.

The effect can be further strengthened by introducing, as well as the plants mentioned above, a large bird bath, a millstone with water trickling over it, a pair of half-barrels with marginal plants, or a low, wide concrete tank with aquatic plants. The gravel which flows between the plants in a natural way like a stream also gives the effect of water. Use ordinary path gravel and do not choose all-white shades – that is too extreme, unless you want a Japanese effect. If you do quartz is good for white gravel.

In this garden I had large terraces laid that sloped down to a wide platform built round an existing willow tree. The willow was trimmed to give a view of the large pool from the house.

The deck in a "wet" garden

I think that one of the most successful elements for patio gardens is stated at the beginning of this chapter. What more could you want if you love water: delightful terraces in sun or shade with a water feature in a formal or natural shape. You can sit there dreamily watching water beetles skating over the water surface, you can hear the frogs at bed-time, and you can enjoy watching dragonflies that cling to the narrow leaves of the bulrush, *Typha angustifolia*.

There is quite a wide choice of aquatics and bog plants, certainly extensive enough to create a spectacular show.

There is no shortage either of marginals with lovely cut or decorated leaves, so something special can certainly be created with decking, a pool, and some attractive garden furniture. I have done it myself many times for clients, usually with great success. I often add a pergola, with wisteria growing over it in the sun or honeysuckle in a shaded place. In the evening you can enjoy the heady fragrance which wafts on the air from the honeysuckle. Of course roses, grapevines, kiwis, and clematis also fit in here. I wouldn't want to be without bamboo, and I wouldn't leave out pots of *Hosta* round the edge of the pool.

The long lines of the jetty lead through reeds to a mysterious place which seems to be heralded by the ornamental grasses.

Left: This narrow path between water and perennials is exciting. It links stone with wood; both go well with water and pond life.

Colour and materials for decking

I used to use deal that had been stained twice for decking. After staining it was then screwed to the joist underneath. Now there is pine pressure-treated with preservative, or hardwood.

Something that is lovely but little used is oak that like other hardwoods goes silver-grey over the years. It is good for at least fifteen years. At Walenburg Castle, where I supervise the maintenance of the particularly fine grounds on behalf on the Dutch Garden Foundation, two beautiful wooden bridges have been built. Both, together with their rails and gates, are made of oak. These have been in intensive use for about thirty-five years and the time has now come for them to be replaced.

These bridges are proof that this native, totally environmentally friendly timber deserves a revival and is a good alternative to hardwoods from the rain forest. It is even suitable for planks themselves; when the surface has deteriorated they can be turned over so that there is a new, clean surface again.

Laying decking

The simplest method to lay decking is to position joists to go under the planks at 60cm (24in) intervals. Make the surface level, then lay the planks flat on top. If you want to make a deck that is removable or to be able to take a section up, construct a set of plank frames

In this garden the owner wanted to have an enormous beech tree taken out in order to let in the light. I decided that one large feature, a U-shaped pool, was needed in its place. A bridge leads to the botanical garden in the inner curve of the U.

which fit exactly between the sleepers. Then a section can be lifted out whenever desired.

If there is a slope and you want to let the deck "float" as far as possible, then you can use another construction method. Square posts are sunk 70 to 80cm (28 to 32in) in the ground. The joists are fixed to them and then the planks are screwed down on them. Keep the distance between the joists at about 60cm (24in), then the planks will not sag.

I designed this front garden with the neighbour's fence as a backdrop. This is openwork with dark-stained plywood palings set close together. The fence gives depth and a certain lightness.

Apart from choosing different methods of construction, you can also choose decking with various surfaces. You can opt for a rough unplaned surface, that will not become slippery very quickly. This is of course not suitable for bare feet. You can also choose grooved pine or treated pine. The wet runs into the grooves so the surface stays dry longer. If this decking is in shadow it can become slippery because of the growth of algae, despite the ridges. One solution to this is to fit strips of dark brown rubber in grooves in the planks. I have had that on my garden steps for about ten years now. The strips, which are not noticeable, have been totally effective and I have never slipped.

To make an original screen you can stack up logs, with or without a small hardwood roof. The result is both rustic and neat.

Geometric pools with luxuriant planting

A geometric pool can perhaps look dull but it doesn't have to be. The straight lines can contrast beautifully with the curved shapes of large-leafed plants.

In many parts of northern Europe we are used to walking, driving, or cycling along straight roads, alongside straight dykes and canals. Is it surprising then that we are fond of geometric pools? But there is also a very different, historical, explanation for them. In old Spanish gardens there are symmetrically-shaped pools which are still admired. In the Alhambra, the palace in the Spanish city of Granada, the pools laid out by the Moors are famous.

There is a rectangular pool between two evergreen hedges whose reflection colours the water green. There is another geometric pool where jets of water cascade into the water from the sides. This pool is at the Generaliffe, the summer palace of the Sultan near the Alhambra.

The spacious, shaded, inner courtyard which contains the pool is surrounded by walls and on either side of the pool there are wide beds filled with luxuriant, scented plants such as jasmine, roses, lemons, and pineapples.

Was it these examples which later led to the construction of geometric pools in many countries and during several centuries? Certainly nothing happens just like that; there is usually a historical reference for a design that has been rediscovered later.

In the Renaissance, but particularly in the baroque in the seventeenth and eighteenth century, long pools or lakes were popular with large landowners because they introduced perspective.

If the line of the water is widthways, then plenty of attention is paid to the planting and the trees. These are round-headed Indian bean trees (Catalpa bignonioides 'Nana').

Personally I am fond of these long lines in enclosed patio gardens too.

Imagine: outside the opening door of the patio house a 3ft (1m) deep terrace is laid out. After that there is a rectangular pool which extends to within 3ft (1m) of the far boundary of the patio. This gives an effect of length. Behind the pool there is *Hosta* and bamboo. To left or right, or on both sides of the pool, there is the terrace, which is thus more or less invisible from the house. In this way you can play with the formal shapes.

L-shaped and U-shaped pools   If you find a simple rectangular pool too dull and for example would like to enclose a terrace on two or even three sides, you will soon come up with an L-shaped or U-shaped pool. Together with a bridge to reach another terrace, a patio can become an exciting arrangement of elements – water, paths, and sitting areas – and in between the luxuriant plantings.

Outstanding ornaments can be displayed in the garden. This is an olive jar from Portugal.

Bulrushes, Typha angustifolia.

31

A border beside a pool

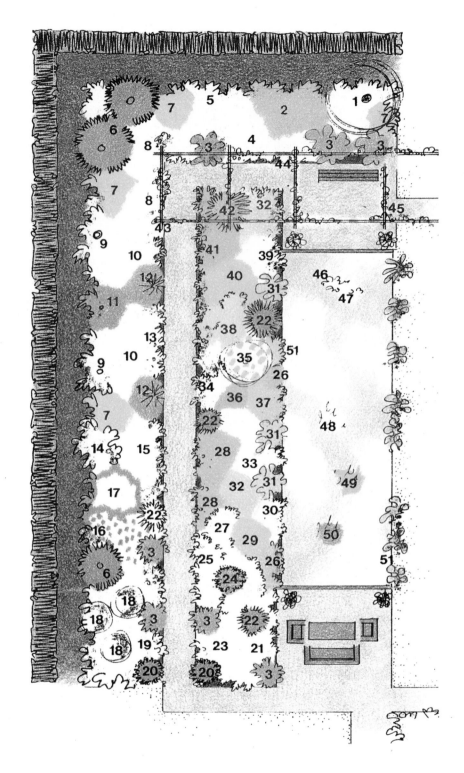

1 *Betula papyrifera*

2 Knap Hill-Exbury azalea 'Golden Flare'

3 *Hedera helix* 'Arborescens'

4 *Skimmia japonica* 'Foremanii'

5 *Rosa* 'Nevada'

6 *Pinus nigra austriaca*

7 *Lamiastrum galeobdolon*

8 *Rhododendron* 'Madam Mason'

9 *Malus floribunda*

10 Knap Hill-Exbury azalea 'Persil'

11 *Aralia elata*

12 *Pennisetum compressum*

13 *Viburnum davidii*

14 *Spiraea arguta*

15 *Iberis* 'Snowflake'

16 *Stranvaesia davidiana*

17 *Stephanandra incisa* 'Crispa'

18 *Amelanchier lamarckii*

19 *Pachysandra terminalis*

20 *Chamaecyparis* tree

21 *Cimicifuga dahurica*

22 *Miscanthus sinensis* 'Gracillimus'

23 *Helleborus niger*

24 *Juniperus*

25 *Anaphalis triplinervis*

26 *Alchemilla mollis*

27 *Rosa* 'Iceberg'

28 *Buphthalmum salicifolium*

29 *Ligularia przewalskii*

30 *Filipendula ulmaria*

31 *Hosta fortunei* 'Aureomarginata'

32 *Kirengeshoma palmata*

33 *Geranium sanguineum* 'Album'

34 *Campanula carpatica*

35 *Malus* 'Golden Hornet'

36 *Lysimachia punctata*

37 *Iris pseudacorus*

38 *Rosa* 'Allgold'

39 *Iris sibirica*

40 *Azalea mollis* 'Adriaan Koster'

41 *Rudbeckia speciosa*

42 *Sinarundinaria murielae*

43 *Rosa* 'Golden Showers'

44 *Lonicera periclymenum*

45 *Wisteria sinensis* 'Alba'

46 *Pontederia cordata*

47 *Sagittaria sagittifolia*

48 *Nymphaea* 'Marliacea Albida'

49 *Nymphaea* 'Marliacea Chromatella'

50 *Typha angustifolia*

51 *Caltha palustris*

Water features in the enclosed garden

Water is not only lovely to look at, it is restful to listen to – particularly if it blots out the sound of traffic.

In southern countries the sound of running water has for centuries attracted people. In northern countries which are blessed with much more rain this sound is less appreciated. There are probably too many days with heavy showers for people to be thrilled at the idea of introducing running water into the patio garden.

Yet that is just prejudice. I have often thought that even in these countries the murmur of water does have a charm and have therefore retained that element in the design for a number of patio gardens.

A water spout can be restful

I once discovered in a shop an old gargoyle that must have come from a Gothic cathedral. It was a remarkable shape: a head that was half human, half lion. Gargoyles were often used on the outer walls and towers of cathedrals, for two reasons. In the first place they served to carry away the water that streamed off the roofs. In the second place they were in the form of terrible demons, intended to scare away the devil who was always trying to gain entry to the Holy of Holies. This is why genuine gargoyles always look like grotesque representations of demons.

The discovery in the antique shop stuck in my memory. When I was faced with clients who lived near a noisy restaurant with a functions room and also had a problem with traffic noise, the idea came to me

I designed this millstone as an alternative to using a stone from a mill. It is made of dark-grey concrete, hollowed out above and below, and it is ideal for birds and for small children, who can splash about by it without any danger of drowning.

to mount the gargoyle in a wall. A lovely wall was built out of old bricks with a slit for the water supply, which was sealed after the copper pipe was put in place. The demon, who for so long had been sitting on a long vertical guttering, was cemented into the wall and connected to the copper pipe. At the bottom of the wall I had a semi-circular cistern built of the same brick with a broad edge that overhung a little. A pump was placed in the cistern so that water could circulate via the copper pipe.

The water could be turned on when there was a lot of noise and also on a quiet Sunday morning. The sound of falling water filled the air; it was clearly audible and visible from the house and from the garden terrace opposite so that all over the garden it was possible to enjoy the pleasant murmur.

I devised a trellis which is covered in clematis and roses against the wall and round the gargoyle. Two containers were placed at the foot of the cistern and planted with hydrangeas and *Hosta sieboldiana* 'Elegans'. All in all it has become a lovely place, something positive has emerged from something negative.

The rest of the garden was refurbished as well, and in the patio area a number of exciting new elements were added. There was a long

If you find an old trough and a nice fountain then a pattern of simple trellis on the wall or, as here, colour shading on the plaster wall is enough to create a restful whole.

formal pool in the lawn, long herbaceous borders along the lawn with hedges and, a little apart, a formal vegetable garden was laid out with low box hedges. This all happened in the old town of Haasdrecht, where this property with its lovely town house is situated.

In this way the completed patio garden, screened from the neighbours, has come to life and offers everything one would wish for in such a garden: beauty, tranquillity, and privacy.

Materials for fountains

Much of what the Egyptian, Greek, and Roman civilizations contributed to fountains has been lost. Fortunately there are, however, ornaments preserved from these civilizations from which copies have been made for centuries. So there are still a number of attractive fountains which have a historic basis.

Terra cotta

For years I had the head of a round-cheeked boy who had pursed his lips into a spout. It was made of terra cotta. Water should come out of the mouth but I had never gone as far as installing a cistern, a pump, and electricity. Apart from the boy, there are terra cotta lion's heads available which spout water.

That is probably the most popular design for a water feature, the lion's head which as well as terra cotta, can be made of bronze, lead,

In this courtyard in Cordoba I was struck by the way the colour of fountain and paving matched. This is restful, although the ornaments may be controversial.

*Among the large-
flowered clematis,
there are many of this
purple with a
beautiful sheen.
Clematis 'Sieboldii' is
mauve-blue, like
'Lasurstern' which is
lighter, the 'Jackmanii
Superba' is purple-
blue, like the 'Lady
Betty Balfour'. 'Etoile
violette' is dark mauve.*

or even sandstone. I recently bought two sandstone lions' heads which have been fixed in the wall of my farmhouse garden to spout water.

Yet these elements are really intended for patio gardens. In a court-yard you can only hear birdsong with perhaps the murmur of neigh-bours or distant traffic. In order to drown those sounds, and also because the sound of running water is pleasant, the water spout has been popular in patios for centuries. Don't delay any longer but go and look for some ornament, cheap or expensive, to achieve this effect tastefully.

Personally I am enthusiastic about lead ornaments. Apart from the lion there are classical ladies available with water coming out of their mouths and a choice of other models.

In a little village I once visited an ancient castle with a courtyard surrounded by walls. It has a great pool in the centre. Against one of the walls enclosing the courtyard iron dolphins, painted dark green, have been set up to spout water. The water falls into a stone cistern and is recirculated to the mouths of the dolphins by a pump. Iron is less expensive than lead or bronze. The statues made of artificial stone are not prohibitively expensive either.

Water circulation

There are various ways of making water flow out of a spout. The simplest is to connect the spout to a pool via a pump. Then the water is taken out of the pool and pumped back in. If you have no pool and don't wish to build one, a water tank either above ground or sunk in the ground can act as a reservoir into which the water falls and can conceal the pump. The tank can be wooden (a barrel), stone (an old feed trough), or brickwork like the one I described in the example earlier.

Stone gutters

Recently from sheer necessity I have designed a spout as simple as it is classical. It consisted of a square-sided rectangular block of stone. On the upper side I had a groove carved. The block is now cemented into the wall. The pipe through which the water is pumped fits exactly in the groove in the stone and the result is a lovely spout which is appropriate for very modern as well as old houses.

Japanese stone or bamboo spouts

In a Japanese-style patio garden there does not have to be water but if there is a place for it, it can add an important element to the atmosphere. To obtain the desired effect it is enough to have water that trickles very slowly or more or less drips from a bamboo pipe.

Although the effect is of the greatest simplicity, it is alas not so simple to achieve as it looks.

In front of the classical summer-house, brought from elsewhere, is a round pool in Rosemary Verney's re-creation of an English cottage garden at Barnsley House. Visitors can look at the pool from the decorative white seats.

Because mains water is too expensive I am only describing water which circulates via a reservoir, a small pump, and a pipe or hose to the bamboo rod. The water falls into a small prefabricated pond, preferably with a minimum depth of 70cm (28in), which also houses the pump. These ponds can be obtained anywhere and they are easy to sink into the ground if there are no tree roots or stumps in the way. If you want the water to fall from the pipe onto a big stone or onto gravel, lay pond liner under the gravel and round the stone in a gulley shape to lead the water to the pond. A pipe can be led upwards from the pond, concealed as far as possible behind bamboo and aquatic plants. A copper pipe is best, but you can use a length of black hose. This then comes up by the bamboo spout, at the back of the bamboo pipe.

In Japan this connection is made with a square block of wood that is fixed to a wooden post. The bamboo pipe has to have the septa at the nodes, which strengthen the bamboo, bored out with a long drill. This needs to be done with the proper tool because the septa are too hard to push through. It is sensible to pull the copper pipe or the hose through the bamboo because bamboo poles often split lengthways and then leaks can occur. Then the system doesn't work any more and the pond has to be topped up constantly as the water leaks from the bamboo pipe. This is all rather involved but it is possible for the handy gardener. The effect is very elegant and restful.

A large wooden deck was my solution to providing a sitting area in this garden. With a pond in front of it the predictability typical of many town gardens was dispelled as if by magic.

Out of a clipped green plant or from a bamboo shrub or a *Camellia* comes a pipe with water dripping softly which fills the patio with a tinkling sound. With a warm glass of sake in the hand you could imagine yourself in the far-eastern gardener's Paradise.

A stone trough as a water feature

Once usually made of granite, now often of artificially weathered and amazingly well-painted concrete, there are troughs and square tanks on the market which can be used as water features. Make sure that there is a lower lip at the side for the water to spill over. Make sure too that there is a basin into which the water can fall, install a pump in it and with a piece of garden hose or a copper pipe lead the water back to the top end of the trough. In Germany, Austria, Switzerland, and other countries with mountains and mountain pasture you see how the water is led to a trough like that which then serves as a drinking place for people and animals. The water is brought through wooden or metal pipes in all kinds of simple but attractive designs.

That is the picture to keep in mind: the atmosphere of the mountains and meadows. Beside the trough you can plant such things as hellebores, monkshood, ox-eye daisies, *Trollius*, and *Campanula* together with a hazel, an elder, or a sweet-briar. In this way you can give your pond a simple but very delicate and elegant character.

One of the most fascinating gardens I know is at the Moorish Alhambra Palace in Granada (Spain). This is the harem garden, filled in summer with red Salvias which glow like fire among the cypresses. The fountain has become a classic and countless copies have been made.

39

A concrete millstone as a water feature

After I had come up against problems many times when I wanted to install a genuine millstone in a garden as a water feature, I went to the drawing board to find a solution. The result can be admired in some experimental gardens in the Netherlands.

These magnificent gardens were saved by my initiative when the owners could no longer afford the upkeep. Now there is a flourishing trust which I helped to set up. The little garden with the millstone serves as an introduction to the new beginning in these model gardens.

Above: The architect Gibbret once took me over his English house, where his wife, a sculptress, had carved this great vase in natural black stone. A narrow pool led the eye to it. Here is a gem of a front garden which has often inspired me.

I want to tell you here what is so special about this millstone made to my design. First of all it is hollowed out so that there is always water in it. This makes it ideal for birds to bathe in and for children, who can play there without any danger of drowning. The colour is anthracite grey so it fits into gardens of any style and mood. The underside of this monster is hollowed out so that the pipes can be concealed and also so that it is light enough to move.

The millstone stands on a grid over a pond, preferably round or square. The water seeps away through cobbles on the grid. Then the pump is installed in the pond and is connected to the centre of the

What is the difference between a swimming pool and a pond? Now both of them may have a black lining. Make a separate area of a swimming pool with grass or spacious terraces and plenty of flowers to hold the attention if you are going to while away the hours there.

stone by a copper pipe. In winter the pump is taken out of the pond and replaced in the spring after it has been cleaned.

In a patio garden the feeling of enclosure can be lessened by similar water features. They make a pleasant sound, reflect the sun, and often attract birds which is a bonus. Birds contribute to the biological control of aphids and caterpillars which, like snails, are always about in the garden.

Even in the safe patio garden the pests are able to come in. Birds are a very attractive and welcome means of control, both visually and audibly.

The Generaliffe, the summer retreat of the Moorish Sultan near his Alhambra Palace in Granada, is built round a rectangular courtyard. In the centre is the famous pool.

The warm colours red, beige, and brown can be toned down with grey-leafed plants. Here the restful shape of the round box shrubs balances the shallow pool surrounded by sandstone and plants.

Differences in level with flights of stairs, steps, and slopes

In order to give a patio more variety, introduce differences in level. These may only be slight: 15cm (6in) deep going down from it and elsewhere 30cm (12in) going up to it can be sufficient.

For example, you can have a 1m (3ft) wide step by the house, outside french windows or sliding doors, that gives access to the garden. You immediately go down 15cm (6in) to a lower terrace. After that you go left or right from this step and up, preferably by more than one step. If you have two steps of 15cm (6in) you go up 30cm (12in) in total. You are now in a separate terrace that can have its own atmosphere. It can feature a pergola, with a vine or scented roses over it. Depending on the size of the area there could be room for a pool between the sitting areas, and for more paths or terraces – perhaps even for grass and plants for enjoyment in summer and winter.

It is not a good idea to start with raised terraces too close to the house, because that makes the area seem smaller when viewed from the house. Beginning with a lower terrace makes the patio more spacious, while different levels in the corner soften the regular shape. Of course there is an almost endless number of ways to introduce differences of level. It is a good plan to disguise the regularity and stiffness of the straight walls and hedges with tall plants by building little walls of wood, brick, or earth up to a certain height against them.

Building or excavating a terrace in one corner at a lower level so that it is invisible from the house can be exciting. It adds interest to

At Castle Gourdon in southern France, Loup de Vianne designed these steps with natural stone risers, filled in with beaten earth. Similar ones can be seen in many other places.

42

what is otherwise a more or less level patio which can all be seen at once.

Brick steps
When you are working with different levels you have to decide what sort of atmosphere you want. If the house, like the walls, is brick, then brickwork steps will fit in. Let the bricks jut out over the edge of the steps so that there is a band of shadow, giving depth when looking upwards. Each step must be designed so that it stays level in winter. That means looking at an expensive, 60cm (24in) foundation. This is necessary on clay, loam, and damp garden soil. If the ground is fairly dry and sandy further down then 30cm (12in) foundations will often be sufficient. The base for the foundation can be built of paving slabs.

For the gardener who is not counting every penny the golden rule is: put in deep foundations, at least 60cm (24in), for brickwork steps. This can of course be expensive, so cheaper bricks are usually used for the foundation, the first facing brick being cemented in at 10cm (4in) below the surface of the lowest brick of the step. Personally I like broad steps. A tread of 60cm (24in) is lovely, you take two steps per tread to descend. Of course steps are much smaller inside the house. An adult's foot measures 25 to 30cm (10 to 12in) long, so that is the minimum size for a step.

This robust sitting area was laid out with sleepers, large slabs and a natural stone table. The tree silhouette, clipped shapes, and wide stone terrace above make this a spacious area with an unexpected wealth of plants.

Stone steps   The simplest way to get materials is to go to a dealer in old building materials and ask for old kerb stones, which are usually made of a durable stone. Sometimes they are brown; more usually they are grey and made of basalt or some other hard stone. These can be used in the patio for steps. There is a problem however; they are very heavy. You will not be able to load them into your Mini, if you still have one, by yourself. When you get them home you will need to ask a strong neighbour to help you put them in place because they do weigh a lot. But they are worth the effort.

In gardens I have designed in Belgium slabs of stone have usually been used for steps. If the step is 15cm (6in) high then a slab 45cm (18in) deep is used, with 30cm (12in) sunk in the ground. It is laid on a sand and cement mixture which is well worked in round the slab to prevent it tipping up. A slab like that then sits in rock-hard mortar and is strong and solid. If you enquire you will find that stone is not cheap. It is worth doing some research to find a source of stone at a reasonable price. Not everyone has the time to look for such places so many people opt for wood, which is relatively cheap.

Wooden steps   In the countries of northern Europe in the Middle Ages and probably much earlier, oak planks were used to make raised beds and to make steps. Turf banks were made too. I digress, but I'll just explain

This town garden which I designed about twenty years ago still looks modern. Curves and straight lines are strongly contrasted in the wooden decking, the millstone, and the wide sleeper steps covered with plants such as Hosta sieboldiana *'Elegans'.*

Opposite page: I extended the narrow terrace behind the house to a sturdy wooden deck.

that a turf bank was a mound of earth which was faced, at least at the front, with wooden planks.

Oak is a suitable and attractive material for steps, although it is never used now. You mostly see hardwood or treated pine.

A wooden step is made as follows: drive or dig in two, preferably square, posts. The plank is fixed against the upper side of the posts. It's as simple as that. Let some evergreens such as ivy, periwinkle, or box grow over the corners to hide the construction. For the tread there is a wide choice of bricks, clay, gravel, and concrete products.

More wood; the ever popular sleepers

I use these as little as possible because they have been overdone. Of course it is silly that something good in itself may be rejected because all the neighbours have used it and you see it on new estates everywhere. That is not a good idea, and those who have gone on using sleepers in spite of their over-popularity are right. Everyone knows the material, so I need only say that under each 15cm (6in) step (which is the thickness of a sleeper laid flat) a second sleeper is used as foundation. Both sleepers are fixed to each other with special rods more than 15cm (6in) long. Sleepers can be stained black, so that they fit in with uncluttered modern shapes and colours.

In this garden I set long steps through the flower border to connect the upper and lower terrace. The willow makes a green sunshade here.

More about wooden steps
For various reasons, I do not like steps that are made of round logs which are driven into the ground vertically side by side, not to mention half-round posts which are sold for this purpose in garden centres. Yet I cannot say that the material is ugly, I have seen logs used effectively for fences and steps, for example. If all the fences, steps, and raised beds are made of them a strong balanced unity can be created and if luxurious planting disguises all the hard lines then there is no problem.

Cobble steps
As an admirer and designer of Japanese gardens I often have steps made of cobbles. Recently I discovered some lovely rounded cobbles in a reddish colour that are extremely suitable for making steps. Choose rounded cobbles with a flat side which can be laid uppermost. You can lay them in a sand and cement mixture to prevent them moving. Broad or narrow steps can be made like this. A narrow step with a cobble diameter of perhaps 40cm (16in) is attractive. You can make the greatest impression by using a number of smaller cobbles laid side by side on the same level and treating the whole as one step.

Raised beds
All the materials mentioned can be used for raised beds. Brick, stone, wood, sleepers, and logs are all suitable. Personally I like brick raised beds but alas they are often too expensive, so

Left: With new buildings you need to know the garden design in order to include it in the building plan. In a situation like that the design must be made early. Here the treads project to give a shadow effect.

47

wood is often used. If higher edges are needed then planks or sleepers are suitable, provided they have been treated with timber preservative.

Slopes Not everyone will want steps, if only to avoid having something to trip over. In hilly areas people are used to meeting slopes where there are differences in level. In the patio garden slopes can link areas at different levels. But does it look attractive? It will depend, for instance, on whether the effect of slopes and raised beds of brick or wood has been designed as a whole. It can work, but it needs thought. And yet, is a sloping brick path necessarily ugly? It is probably unusual, because in enclosed patios the tendency is generally to build steps.

There are some good reasons for using slopes. One is that some people have difficulty in walking, and another is that some have to garden from a wheelchair. It is essential to find a suitable way of incorporating height differences in their gardens.

If slopes have to be walked on it is sensible to use a non-slip surface. Bricks can be laid with ridges, that is the upper surface of each brick is laid level, and therefore at a slight angle to the slope. This method can also be used on steep drives. Gravel is less suitable; feet can slip

Here a combination of materials creates a striking effect. Terrace, steps, path, and fence are united by a profusion of perennials and roses.

Opposite page: By using water you can have lovely "seaside" weekends in the garden. This pool built out of sleepers is sturdy and longlasting, even when time for gardening is limited. The stepping stones are also made of sleepers.

on it. That can happen with wet cobbles too, so many people choose concrete cobbles or bricks which have a rough surface. To stabilize the soil line the sides of these paths with greenery and flowering plants that root well such as *Pachysandra*, *Vinca*, ivy, and *Campanula*.

Different kinds of step form an airy flight here with wood and light natural stone leading down to the brick terrace.

You can also hide a flight of steps among greenery and flowering plants so that each step is a discovery.

Verandahs as enclosures

One garden feature that can be very attractive is the verandah – and it is one that you may not have considered.

A patio is a separate area of the garden. It is protected by walls, fences, or tall hedges. It has a floor and a "roof" that is basically open to the sky. The overall effect can be rather box-like so shrubs, trees, or large-leafed plants need to be introduced to liven it up. There must also be shaded areas in order to add interest. A verandah can contribute to this enlivening effect and it has the advantage that because it is built and not growing it will always keep its original dimensions.

With a verandah you can make a transition between house and garden that is rigid and architectural. Always choose hardwood or treated timber for the verandah pillars, which must be able to take sufficient weight, and preferably use good, treated timber for the cross-members.

I always want to continue "living in the garden" without getting wet when there is light rain, so for me parasols or covered verandahs are very important.

Building a verandah is often an involved business. It is sensible to employ a builder to put up the pillars, cross-beams, and roof. The roof can be made of dark hardwood or it can be translucent, made of wired glass. In the latter case the construction must be sturdy

This verandah has been placed at an angle and roofed with tiles so that a splendid area has been created for working, sitting, and exhibitions. The white posts match the lovely white house. There is a beautiful garden with a pool, flowers, vegetables, and an orchard.

enough to take the weight of the glass. Remember too that it may have to withstand snow. This is another reason for having it properly built.

A pointed roof with wooden tiles

I once visited a garden where a verandah had been built in the Japanese style. There was a pool in front of it. The floor was wood, as was the pointed roof, which even had wooden tiles. It was made of treated pine, which eventually becomes greenish grey.

The pointed roof gave a great feeling of space; it is certainly an idea worth copying. In America wooden tiles have been used for a long time but they are not so common in Western Europe. I have seen them in Japan, made of *Cryptomeria* timber which is used as a hardwood there.

Eventually lichens grow on the tiles and within a short time a roof made of them will look weathered and appear to be completely integrated with nature.

Another possible material which is not often used for a verandah is iron. Particularly with a modern house an austere construction can continue the modern style into the garden. You can design it yourself but do ask a specialist to make it for you.

A round beam on two round posts makes a first-rate pergola.

This garden has been made out of part of a driveway. I designed the layout and the planting. The owners built the shed, which determines the shape of the verandah. The low wall for sitting on divides the flower garden from the dining area.

52

Arbours and parasols

In an arbour and under a parasol we can sit in the shade, or, more important in our climate, stay outside but dry in the rain if the temperature is still pleasant.

If you want to have your own arbour you need a large garden or an outdoor room with a hedge round it. It is something that is relatively easy to achieve. One option is a light construction, for instance using iron.

Just think of the famous white garden at Sissinghurst. It is a patio garden that is enclosed partly by walls and partly by high hedges. In the centre there is an iron arbour, open to the sky, but with a living "roof" of white roses. Everybody who sees it is captivated by it, and it has inspired many people to put up an arbour for themselves, covered by climbing plants.

In a corner or in the middle of the patio an iron construction can become a shaded arbour with white or purple wisteria trained over it, or deep pink roses, or a freely flowering *Clematis montana*. Whether or not a closed summer-house fits in a patio garden has yet to be seen. Perhaps you know a good example, but I cannot really imagine it and I prefer the idea of a veranda which reflects the lines of the house with its vertical pillars and horizonal cross-members.

Parasols   In Italy they are used in the markets to keep the sun off the wares, those great wooden parasols which are covered with cream canvas. The fact that they can also function as umbrellas only makes these

This little roof of rattan cane turns grey in the rain, which looks lovely beside the muted colours in this garden. It is not to shelter under in the rain or strong sunlight.

great light elements more attractive. They took time to reach our private gardens but now there is no stopping them and they are for sale in all sorts of designs and price ranges. Do take account of the wind, because you don't want the parasol ending up on top of your prize delphiniums. There are three possibilities.

Firstly, you can sink a pipe in the ground and fill the space round it with cement. Put plenty of grit under the open pipe to prevent it filling up with water, because that will do the foot of the parasol no good.

A second way of anchoring it is to use a black or dark-green iron plate with a tube welded to it. This plate will give sufficient breadth at the foot of the parasol.

Thirdly, there are heavy, solid tables with a round hole in the top to hold the parasol. For extra security the foot of the parasol should rest in an iron holder under the table.

That of course applies to the heavy Italian wooden parasols with a wide canvas cover. For many years the famous Belgian restaurant Scholteshof had the whole of its terrace restaurant covered with these parasols so that each table stood under one. When it rained

Facing page: Hand-painted parasols of oiled paper are all the rage in America. They are available in many colours, or you can get busy with the paint brush. They are not rain-proof but they do make a splendid summer picture.

A restful garden, everything here is under control, healthy, and well cared for. Drinking tea here must provide refreshment for body and soul.

Sandstone slabs are
laid over the edge of
the swimming pool in
this beautifully
thought-out design.
Here the swimming
pool looks like a small
lake, strengthened by
the use of black liner
instead of the
usual blue.

diners could stay under cover so that only the waiters got wet. Anyone who wants to eat out in the open air but would prefer not to get wet, can put up a parasol near the house. The only problem is with heavy rain, when water coming off the cover splashes up. That is why my favourite place out of doors remains a covered terrace adjoining the house.

Fortunately for those of us who cannot carry heavy weights there are many types of parasol on the market. They come in all colours and in light-weight designs. If it is windy you must have a solid support even for a small parasol to stop it blowing over. The famous flower painter Maria Hofker always clamps a parasol to her chair, which looks lovely.

That brings me to another possibility. Each chair can have its own parasol. Whatever you choose, do not forget to consider the colour of the plants near the parasol and the terrace. You can try to choose a colour that makes an "extension" of the colour of the plants. But you can also choose a contrast. The choice of colour is important, because a parasol is a large area which can "kill" the surrounding planting.

This post and the diagonal supports give an attractive rural effect. You can cover a pergola beautifully with wisteria, grapevine, Clematis montana, and some scented roses. Within a couple of years it will be almost completely covered.

56

The patio garden with perennials

Nowadays many garden owners do not have very much time for gardening. Perennial plants, in pots or in the ground, are a good choice for people with limited time.

The dream of many patio owners is to have a carpet of flowering plants among terraces, paths, and other features such as ponds. You will see that this is not difficult to achieve. It is important too to have a pretty garden in winter. Evergreen plants must be planted in places where they are clearly visible. There are some ideas in the next chapter.

There are many flowering plants but very few go on flowering for months. So I mix roses with perennials, since modern roses are in bloom from June to October. *Geranium endressii*, a pink-flowered perennial 40cm (16in) high, also has a long season, like *Sedum* 'Herbstfreude', which flowers from July to October. There are many plants like that, such as the ground-cover plant *Campanula portenschlagiana*, which has a long season especially if you remove the dead flowers in good time.

Yet most plants flower for a month or six weeks at the most. So the flowering succession needs to be kept in mind. Therefore my advice is to choose perennials with attractive leaves – which are variegated or spotted, have a fine structure (fern-like for example), or are very large and therefore striking. Examples are *Hosta*, with large, oval leaves; *Darmera* (*Peltiphyllum*), which has large, round leaves with a lobed edge; and *Ligularia*, which has yellow flowers. *Cimicifuga*,

Grey perennials, such as this bunnies' ears, Stachys byzantina, *emphasize the red of the bricks. The grey* Lavendula, *which is a low shrub, is less bright, giving a softer contrast.*

57

Rosa 'Madam Hardy'
rises here above a
mixture of perennials:
the pale-pink
Campanula lactiflora
'Loddon Anna', the
lemon-yellow
Alchemilla mollis
and in the left fore-
ground Eryngium
giganteum.

which flowers from July to October, has fine leaves which are always lovely. The same applies to *Astilbe* and *Geranium clarkei* 'Kashmir White', which has beautiful white flowers for a short time. *Pulmonaria*, at least the most usual cultivars, have spotted leaves. Other plants with variegated leaves are *Brunnera*, with silver markings; the perennial forget-me-not, and *Hosta*, which can have white or gold margins. Don't forget silver-grey, which is dealt with in a later chapter.

Have something flowering in the garden and use perennial bulbs for early spring colour, and ornamental onions for summer interest. Autumn colour can be achieved with the autumn crocus and the perennial hardy cyclamen.

A weekly visit to a well-stocked garden centre or a good open-air market will show you that the range of perennials is almost limitless.

Always take a notebook and a camera is very useful. Photograph what is flowering at that particular time, make notes and then make your choice. If you are not given to research then ask an expert to make you a design and a planting plan. Then you will avoid wasting money on the wrong plants. Personally I enjoy a weekly visit to garden centres all over the country, looking for common or unusual plants.

In the classical
herbaceous border the
lower plants are at the
front with the taller
ones behind. Here
Sedum *'Herbstfreude'*
is in the foreground.
This plant becomes
pinkish to brick-red
later and goes well
with autumn-
flowering anemones.
The yellow Achilleas
are like flash lights,
emphasizing the
lighter shades and
making the darker
shades more muted.

Behind a modern house there was a boring lawn with tall, columnar coniferous trees on a small rise in the centre. At a stroke the large pool livened it up. New sitting areas were laid out with views of the pool and the new perennials from all sides. A pergola was built over a terrace, so there is some shade in what is otherwise a sunny garden, which has now become very exciting.

Creating an exciting garden

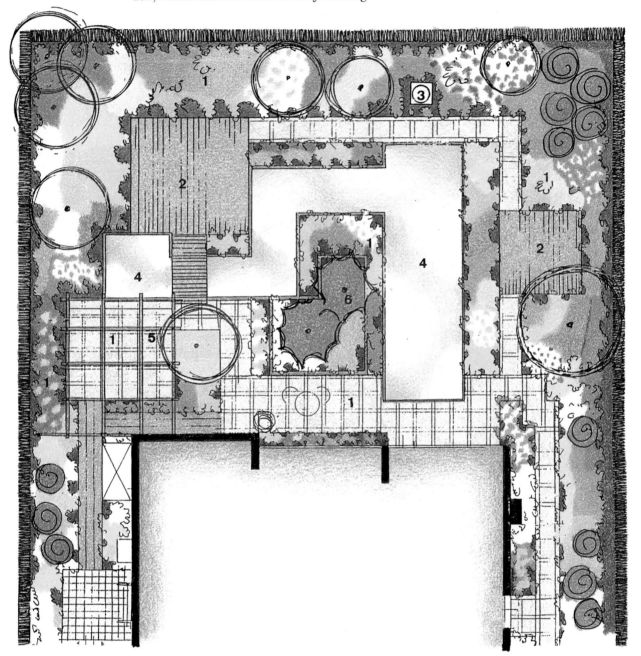

1   original slabs combined with brick
2   wooden decks
3   modern sculpture on a pedestal
4   plastic pool with wooden surround
5   hardwood pergola with vine trained over it
6   original pillar-shaped conifers
7   perennials in blue shades

The evergreen patio

A fellow garden designer once said in an interview: "Anyone can make a nice garden in the summer; the problem is creating a beautiful garden for the winter."

This is very true and a good starting point for planting your own patio garden.

I usually begin by putting in a tree or a large shrub when I have an enclosed area to plant. When that is fixed, then round this tree, bare in winter, I group green plants such as hellebores (*Helleborus foetidus* or *H. lividus corsicus*). Then come box bushes or evergreen shrubs such as *Viburnum davidii*, which has white flowers and purple berries. It grows to about 50cm (20in). For a taller feature I usually choose a holly for its berries or bamboo for its decorative and rustling evergreen stems. That introduces some movement, which is very important in a static, enclosed space. Only when this main shape is in place, probably filled in with a low evergreen hedge or a terrace along a path to break up the space, are other plants added, preferably evergreen ones. These can be *Epimedium* (low), *Tiarella* (low, white), *Waldsteinia* (low, yellow), *Asarum* (low, yellow), *Vinca* (low, blue), and so on.

If you want to cover the terrace further then stand box mini-balls in pots round, with ivy that can hang over the edges. Put the box and ivy in black plastic containers which you can sink in the ground in the spring. In winter put them in attractive terra cotta pots, which will then not shatter if the compost freezes in the inner pots.

For golden margins on blueish Hosta *leaves choose* Hosta sieboldiana 'Frances Williams'. *Here it is the leaf of* Hosta sieboldiana 'Elegans' *which is turning colour at the end of the summer. In the background* Ligularia dentata 'Othello'.

Surfaces between ground-cover plants

It is not difficult to fill a garden: plant shrubs, sweet briar, acanthus, and masses of tall, spreading perennials and the patio will soon become a jungle – which is fine if you dream of living in the rain forest...

Those who like space will have to be very careful with tall, spreading plants in the patio. For them it is important to place just a few features in the space. These can then emerge from low-growing ground-cover plants. Fortunately there is plenty of choice. Of the shrubs there is ivy, *Euonymus fortunei* 'Carrierei', and several trailing roses such as *Rosa macrantha* 'Raubritter.' There is even more choice among the perennials: *Alchemilla mollis* reaches a height of 30 to 40cm (12 to 16in) in flower; the leaf is large. There are many low-growing species and varieties of *Campanula*, while *Vinca*, *Pachysandra*, *Tiarella*, and *Ajuga* are just a few of the well-known perennials which can cover the ground. If you want to create a restful atmosphere then plant large groups of one species. Put these large groups next to each other and then here and there add a specimen plant – not too many – and keep the design asymmetrical, which gives a natural look. Pay attention to leaf shape and the colour of flowers and foliage; remember too that the time of flowering is important. For example: begin with a large group of *Waldsteinia ternata*, it has yellow flowers in summer; followed by *Alchemilla mollis*; then a group of *Helleborus lividus corsicus*. Like *Waldsteinia* this last is evergreen and has greenish-yellow flowers. For blue shades plant *Ajuga reptans*, May-flowering; then *Campanula poscharskyana*, which first flowers in June; after which dwarf Michaelmas daisies provide an autumn show.

This concrete was left when a barn was demolished. It provided a base for pots and the matted, green grass is a bonus.

In Mediterranean countries black and white water-worn, rounded pebbles are often used for paving. This has a pomegranate design. We sometimes see similar patterns in northern Europe.

You can have an abundance of white: *Iberis sempervirens* 'Snowflake' flowers early in spring, after which *Tiarella cordifolia* and *T. wherryi* show white candles which will follow each other right through until the autumn. There are more white trailing roses: *Rosa* 'Snowballet', for example, while there is also the evergreen white-flowered *Pachysandra*.

In pink you can choose the early, pink *Helleborus orientalis*, after which *Geranium endressii* makes her appearance. For sunny corners there are maiden pinks, soapworts (pink), and *Sedum spurium* 'Schorbuser Blut'; while for autumn colour there are dwarf Michaelmas daisies in beautiful shades of pink and purple. Plant them in big groups. If you do not want flowers, you can cover the ground in green shades with, for example, *Hosta*, Christmas roses, and the ornamental grass *Pennisetum compressum*. There is also the low-growing grass *Festuca gautieri* which forms clumps. It is beautiful as an ornamental and needs to be planted in large groups.

Lavender and *Santolina* are somewhat tender plants in cold, damp areas. Furthermore they need to be pruned at the right time. For me, on clay in Zeeland in the Netherlands, that is the end of April, when I have to cut them back to 10 to 15cm (4 to 6in) with the shears. This ensures the best new growth and flowers, after that I can enjoy the very decorative grey shapes all through the winter.

Chippings have sharp edges, not rounded ones. They are available in very many colours.

Facing page: This lovely building houses the Secretariat of the Dutch Garden Foundation, dedicated to the conservation of notable private gardens which are open to the public. You can phone for information on 00 31 20 6235058 or visit it yourself. You approach it up the gravel path between the dwarf box hedges.

Surfaces with gravel and chippings

Anyone who likes rough textures and is thrilled by beaches, river banks, and everything that reminds them of warmth and the south will enjoy large clumps of lavender in gravel, or trailing roses in ochre-yellow chippings. The atmosphere of the south adds to a feeling of well-being, enhanced by warm brick walls.

If the walls of your patio are white then choose white gravel such as quartz, or just dark-grey chippings with silver-grey ground cover such as lavender. Some clays, which are used as a surface, are ochre-coloured. To have all yellow shades with these looks nice, and so are the shades of green of *Hosta*, *Pachysandra*, *Waldsteinia*, and lady's mantle. Lay a mixture of small yellowish stones set with clay in a layer 20cm (8in) thick and you will have an almost maintenance-free surface. Gravel can be used, too, and needs virtually no maintenance. For this a honeycomb grid of hard plastic is put down on a geo-textile membrane where the gravel is to be laid. The walls are 4 to 5cm (1 to 2in) high. Very fine shingle is spread over the grid. Because of the grid you can walk on the gravel and even take wheelbarrows or drive cars across it without it sinking. Gravel, clay, and chippings are all relatively cheap, easy to use, and distinctive.

Anyone who likes to walk bare-foot will want brick or paved terraces, but where it isn't necessary the surfaces I have discussed, which are less often used, are well worth considering.

I made some changes to the planting in the garden of the Prince Bernard Fund in Amsterdam. The shape remains the same with gravel as a surface round the flower-beds. The blue leaf belongs to Hosta tardiana *'Halcyon'.*

Topiary

If you have a garden full of shrubs and conifers which are out-growing the space there are two possibilities: thin them out or clip them into topiary shapes.

In this Jardin d'Amour in the Van Buren Museum in Brussels the light-green topiary shapes are box, the dark green are Taxus baccata.

The first possibility is to thin out the shrubs by removing some or pruning them hard back, that is almost to the ground. With many kinds that can be done every four or five years without problems. It can, however, only be done with a few conifers, such as *Taxus –* yew – and it is not usual.

The second possibility is to clip the shrubs into round shapes. That can give something exciting and you can discover new possibilities in your own garden. At any rate, as I find out every time, you can succeed in bringing order out of the chaos of branches and creating a beautiful design of rounded shapes. I saw this happen for the first time in a garden which I was designing at the back of a large town house.

The client was an artist who makes large wall hangings out of all kinds of yarn for banks, universities, airlines, and museums. She knows about design, although she could not work out the arrangement of her garden, hence my involvement. The house was tall, the garden was low. I designed great, sweeping, wooden terraces, stained black, which were set at an angle to each other. There was grass along the right-hand side, with a pool and a huge weeping willow. On the left there was a single conifer. There I planted a mass of oleaster against a grey wall. After several years this grey mass was so wild that she asked the gardener to prune each plant into a round shape. The result was a beautiful rippling landscape of grey evergreens. I learned a lot from it. Since then I have pruned all shrubs which have become too big into round shapes, as well as conifers that can stand it. It is obvious that you must not overdo this; it must not become tasteless and must be limited to a few groups of single round shapes. They then become the pauses in the symphony of the garden.

I once designed a garden in stages. Alongside the path into the garden which was lined with an abundance of flowering plants, there were groups of shrubs which had been clipped into rounded shapes. This gave a restful feel and some winter interest. There were also low spheres of box, like plover's eggs, laid in amongst the *Geranium*, *Hosta*, and other leaf shapes, and very deliberately kept free from any leaves which would spoil the perfect egg shape. Elsewhere in the garden shrubs were clipped into balls; one instance was the *Ligustrum* which was planted as a shrub border and had got out of control. The *Ligustrum* bushes were clipped into cones, a popular shape in topiary. They give rhythm and dramatic form to an otherwise unremarkable shrub border.

Ideal evergreen shrubs for topiary

All hollies are good for topiary, provided you begin when the shrubs are still young. Holly has one disadvantage: if the shrubs become bare low down they have difficulty sprouting again. In practice they hardly ever sprout from below, so once a bare holly, always a bare holly. There are three possibilities. You can either grow a holly as a

Facing page: Anyone who likes topiary shapes will prune the wisteria in summer and take off all the straggling stems, so that these round (or flat) shapes make a decorative edging to gate, fence or wall.

Pleached limes, forming a hedge on stilts, stand in front of an established beech hedge. A low hedge was planted between the trunks of Tilia.

Ivy can be trained into a hedge over wire-netting, against an earth bank, or against posts. So the gleaming box parterre can be finished off with an equally gleaming hedge. You can also make shiny hedges of Lonicera pileata *and* Lonicera nitida, *as well as of the dwarf* Ilex crenata.

standard, in which case you cut off all the lower branches, which can be attractive. Then you can plant ground cover under it so you can see through underneath the bush, which gives a feeling of space. Or a second possibility is to cut the shrub down to within about 50cm (20in) of the ground and hope that it will sprout again. You run the risk of having a bare stem for the first year. Thirdly, you can plant a small holly in the gap, a solution that works well. Choose the same species or variety, of course.

Next to holly, box is the most popular evergreen shrub. There are more than eighty forms of box, so making a collection of them is a life's work. At the Langley Boxwood Nursery, near Liss, Hampshire in England, however, there are more than sixty species and varieties available. If you have the space you could plant them all.

Box can be clipped, although there can be problems in pruning old, straggling bushes into a good shape. Bare old branches do not sprout readily so, as with holly, there are the three possibilities of growing as standard, cutting right back, or planting in the gap. Apart from round shapes you can also clip them into cubes. I like large cubes or small ones placed as architectural features among a profusion of colour and foliage. They are very suitable for the transition from house to garden, appropriate for the patio garden.

Osmanthus heterophyllus looks rather like holly but it grows more slowly. It has a beautiful leaf, decorative and indented. It clips well

By bringing together all kinds of ornaments in shades of grey under a huge tree an air of mystery has been created. Box in a pot is suitable for the winter and for the serious, sombre character of this design. The shapes recall old Italian gardens.

Bay trees in tubs are clipped in summer.

into lovely round shapes. It is less suitable for hedges. Like box and holly there are variegated forms available.

Lonicera pileata and *L. nitida* are both suitable for topiary. They have tiny leaves. *L. pileata* reaches 1.4m (4ft6in), *L. nitida* 60cm (24in) if unclipped.

Prunus laurocerasus has leaf forms varying from pointed to round. They are all suitable for topiary and make good balls. With them too, you must begin early. Apart from *P. laurocerasus* my favourite in this family is *P. lusitanica*, which has long, narrow leaves and can be clipped into shapes. It is ideal for balls which are quite high, pointed shapes, and anything else you fancy.

Apart from these evergreens there are also grey-leaved shrubs. The shrub *Eleagnus x ebbingii* is one of them. It produces long shoots that must be clipped regularly or the shape will be lost in no time. Unfortunately it is sometimes attacked by a virus which can leave bare patches that take time to fill in. This is really the only true evergreen, "evergrey" shrub which is hardy in northern Europe. There are some more or less grey-leafed *Viburnum* species, such as *V. x burkwoodii* which has white flowers in early spring. The secret is to prune them into a ball immediately after flowering, and then clip the young shoots during the summer. This avoids cutting out the old wood on which it flowers.

In effect you can clip these shrubs to whatever shape you wish. Some will have to be clipped heavily, others less.

Shrubs with grey leaves

Salix repens nitida, which is silver-grey, remains dwarf. *Eleagnus angustifolia* is also silver-grey, like *Pyrus salicifolia*. The last two are tall shrubs. You can obtain unexpected effects with these silver-grey shrubs by clipping them several times a year into round shapes. The *Eleagnus* does not belong among these because it is only grey on the underside and, besides, it keeps its leaves.

Shrubs with green leaves

Beech, *Fagus sylvatica*, is green in summer, has bare twigs in winter, and is suitable for topiary. The hornbeam, *Carpinus betulus*, has light-green shoots early in the year and in winter is 60 per cent bare. The other 40 per cent has dry, brown leaves.

Hawthorn, *Crataegus monogyna*, has white blossom, comes into leaf early, and has red berries until late winter. Otherwise it is bare and can be pruned. In fact, all the hedging shrubs are suitable for clipping into balls.

Forsythia can be clipped and will still flower. Before you choose *Forsythia*, remember that it must be pruned. It flowers early and for the rest of the year has, dull, almost bare twigs. Of course you can put other plants in front of it to disguise the bare branches.

Growing box in pots can mean starvation for the shrubs so nurture them with water and fertilizer. In dry periods black plastic or terra cotta saucers can be placed under the pots. Remove them during wet spells.

Box prefers to grow in the ground. If you want to grow these balls in pots then they must be fed every week to produce specimens like these home-grown ones.

There are some shrubs which are not suitable for topiary such as elder which is leafless below, as is *Buddleia*. *Spiraea* shrubs are suitable, but in practice they are infrequently clipped into shapes. The leaves are usually fine and decorative compared with *Ligustrum*, beech, and oleaster.

You sometimes see original ideas for hedges in a garden such as one I saw where the fine-leafed *Stephanandra incisa* 'Crispa' had been used. This is lovely in a small group or as a single specimen in a patio; it grows to 50cm (20in), with fine green leaves. The wood is reddish-brown and very striking in winter. This shrub, which is mostly used as ground cover, had been clipped into a neat hedge. Again it showed off the beautiful, fine leaves to advantage.

In your patio experiment with rounded shapes and let them increase in height from the walls to a large ball by the terrace. The summer sun will colour the wood and make a very attractive feature.

Where plants and architecture have been combined for centuries, the plants must be pruned or they will take over. As long as there have been gardens the climbers, the hedges, shrubs, and specimen plants have been clipped into fantastic shapes.

Following page: The maximum use is made of the walls of the patio by letting them become overgrown, then positioning in front of them containers overflowing with plants.

71

The oriental patio

It is amazing how in two more or less separate parts of the world two totally different, but both equally exciting, gardening traditions have developed.

In the Far East people have recognized that for vegetables and special ornamental plants it is necessary to erect walls, hedges, and fences against wild animals and human greed. Yet within that outline people have sought a connection with nature – the landscape – by their use of materials, choice of plants, and design. Since in nature there is hardly any symmetry and asymmetry is the rule, the design of the eastern garden became asymmetric. There are many ways of giving an impression of asymmetry. In the first place there have been many books on the subject, for example about the old Chinese gardens and the Japanese gardens which were inspired by them, but which have otherwise developed in a completely different direction, towards the Zen art of gardening. This more abstract approach to design and symbolism has not taken place in China. Since many patios are laid out as gardens these distant gardens are a fascinating source of inspiration for us. A Chinese garden usually begins with a paved entrance courtyard.

Chinese courtyards In China a great deal of thought is given to the paving of the entrance courtyard, which is sometimes laid out in a chequerboard pattern with baked grey tiles combined with pebbles. There are often curved terra cotta bricks which look like roof tiles on edge. They are mostly grey with some reddish-purple. A single decorative plant may be placed against a wall as a fanciful feature. A *Nandina domestica*, for example, is very suitable with its dark-green, decorative leaves and

Water lilies have been introduced into Japan and are popular in parks and royal gardens such as the Meije Park in Tokyo.

Facing page: From a plain tea-house there is a view over this pool. The moon is reflected in the pool when people seek the tranquillity and order of the tea ceremony in the evening.

74

red berries following the white flowers. Beyond the entrance there is often a patio alongside which people live in buildings like pavilions with a lot of trelliswork in ox-blood red. You may see strangely pruned trees and shrubs, such as a standard *Camellia* or a clipped maple. The tree peony, *Paeonia arborescens*, is popular for its spring flowers.

People try not to use grass and to keep the paths narrow. These paths are roofed over so that there is protection from sun and rain in summer. Those are good ideas to imitate, at least if you have a feel for oriental design. The effect can soon become gimmicky if there are too many stones, ugly pools and the wrong choice of plants. Always be sparing with stones. Never choose white gravel, always keep to muted shades for chippings, pebbles, and tiles.
Round shapes of camellias, yew, holly, and box look lovely with the pebbles because the shape of the pebbles is repeated in the evergreen shrubs.

Take that as the starting point for the arrangement of the patio. Then add specimen plants such as maple, *Magnolia kobus* as a large shrub, and *Prunus* as a shrub or tree. *Pinus cembra* is very suitable as a specimen tree with its evergreen, curious shapes, and another possibility is *Cryptomeria*. This can be either *Cryptomeria japonica*, a

In Ireland I discovered this trompe l'œil Chinese garden, with bonsai in brightly coloured Chinese dishes.

forest giant which can grow to a great height, or a lower shrub or tree variety such as *Cryptomeria japonica* 'Dacrydioides'. *Cryptomeria japonica* 'Globosa Nana', which is a rounded, low-growing form, is fully hardy.

The pool   In many Chinese patio gardens of any size you will see a pool, commonly with craggy rocks round it. To be honest I sometimes find these rather cluttered, so I usually opt for a simple pool. I never choose a rectangular one. It must never be completely round either – that would be too artificial. I think a kidney or S-shape is ideal, with some stones here and there. Group the stones together at the back with one single stone on its own that can be seen from the house.

Azaleas can be planted beside the stones and round the pool; choose the small-leafed Japanese azaleas and prune them well so that they remain small. Choose azaleas in one or two colours that go together, but which flower in succession or have different shades of one colour. Choose grey concrete slabs for the paths; dark grey or charcoal grey is especially attractive, or even a blue-grey natural stone. Spread neutral, greyish chippings everywhere else, to give a restful uniformity. A geo-textile membrane is laid under the chippings to prevent roots coming through. For the terraces choose grey, natural-stone slabs or dark-grey concrete slabs, preferably small ones.

I created the simplicity which people see in the Japanese tea garden with my own materials. I look for the combination with water, here a stone plate over which water flows into a pool. The rim prevents water running over the side.

77

Wooden decks do not belong in Chinese gardens but pavilions with trelliswork do. They can look lovely against a wall near the pool or among the *Prunus* or maples.

The Japanese patio garden

If you want a great contrast with the Chinese garden then choose a so-called "dry" water garden. This consists of a dry garden where gravel gives the effect of water. In principle it is simple to lay out. Any area not paved or planted is underlain by a geo-textile membrane on which white quartz gravel is spread. You can also use fine white or sand-coloured grit, which can more easily be raked into patterns.

That is what happens in Japan. Flowing water is chosen as a theme and lines are raked in the grit in wavy and flowing lines using a coarse wooden rake. Then the grit looks like water. On my visits to many of these dry water gardens I have seen that the effect works.

A "wet" water garden

With a wet water garden there is usually a height difference, so in your patio you would need to build a low wall against a wall or fence opposite the living room, preferably in a natural, asymmetrical shape. At the bottom of the wall set a stone that water can flow over via a pipe and small pump. The water can then flow into a pool and be recycled. Plant the slope with clipped, rounded box, azalea, and yew. At the top

The Nanzen-i Temple in Kyoto has many gardens, most of them surrounded by white walls. This is the first great courtyard where along one side grow clipped evergreens with moss under them which tries to cover the gravel. Daily raking prevents this.

and halfway down there must be some specimen shrubs such as Japanese maple, *Camellia*, and *Prunus* so that the slope is rounded off. Japanese irises, *Iris kaempferi*, grow by the pool. There must be further round-clipped shrubs on the slope. Ferns are suitable along the pool edge, beside an isolated stone for instance.

Keep the overall picture calm and choose stones in muted colours, for example dark grey or dark brown, otherwise they will be too obtrusive. For the wet water garden choose azalea, maple, *Prunus*, bamboo, and clipped round shapes of – among others – *Ilex crenata*, which is popular in Japan.

Anyone who is fond of topiary will create "clouds" of green here. Just buy a multi-stemmed *Ilex crenata*. Prune two or three branches free and train them up bamboo canes in an asymmetrical shape. This takes quite a time. The branches can then be made to grow out to form a kind of fan. Then at the top of each branch clip a flattened sphere which must be shaped like a cloud. The height of the clouds must vary and they must not be touching. When there are three clouds then one shoot can be allowed to grow on and the cloud shape can be repeated. They must 'float' or sit asymmetrically on the branches. Conifers such as yew do well like that, they can be trained and clipped extremely effectively. Other holly varieties and *Osmanthus* can easily be clipped and shaped too.

Water, even if only in the form of a small pool, creates a peaceful atmosphere in the garden. Not much space is needed to enjoy the fish and the often magnificent aquatics.

Never use variegated forms; they are not suitable – not even the red Japanese maples. These only turn red in the autumn.

The transparent character of this water garden gives an authentic Japanese atmosphere.

Japanese terraces

In a patio grey natural stone slabs are suitable. Dark-grey concrete slabs are a cheaper alternative. I usually make wooden decks, which 'float' above the plants or the gravel. I use wood because in Japan people often sit on the wooden floor of a verandah at a house or temple and contemplate the garden. In Japan where the rainfall is heavy, stone slabs are often used on covered terraces instead of wood. But you may not want to be quite so orthodox.

A Japanese teahouse or covered terrace

I once designed a Japanese garden for a large patio at offices in Denmark. There was a pool and a number of wooden terraces where the staff could sit in the sun, and for visitors there was a true Japanese arbour which I designed. It was built a little above the level of the garden to keep the underneath of the wood dry. The floor of the teahouse was wooden. One advantage of the roofs of Japanese teahouses is that they always extend so far that the sun does not shine through the sliding doors that enclose the central area. The rain cannot get in either unless there is a storm.

The sliding walls are of trelliswork construction with paper stuck over it. In northern Europe that would last no time so I had the outside of

the sliding walls glazed. Within the walls the floorcovering is fine tatami matting, made of plaited rice stalks, ideal for walking or sitting on. The matting is built up from several layers so it is springy. Sake is available here as an alternative to tea. Demonstrations of ikebana (Japanese flower arranging) are given here too. After some searching I found the black roof tiles for the tea house. I made the steps up to the high wooden verandah out of black granite. The whole finally became a lovely feature which works perfectly.

For the patio or conservatory: a water-filled barrel gives you the opportunity to put in a few lovely aquatic plants and enjoy their flowers.

Anyone who wants to attempt this in their own patio should first of all read various books about this type of construction and study the photographs in particular. If need be, seek advice to avoid building something that does not work. It is better to build a covered verandah or restrict yourself to a simple little roof than to have an expensive failure.

A Japanese-style pergola

In Japan I often saw pergolas based on round, brown posts with round cross-members. On top of these bamboo slats and sticks were placed on each other, each layer lashed at right angles with black sisal. You can copy this using treated round poles, or square posts and beams 8 x 8cm (3 x 3in). The bamboo beams, which must be quite thick, come on top, and for the final layer use the largest size of bamboo cane and lash them with black sisal. To be fair, I usually use copper wire and then wrap the decorative rope round it.

The aim is to nail or screw as little as possible in order to spare the wood "pain". The souls of the ancestors can after all return to a tree. So by tradition no nails are driven into wood. Purple or white wisteria can be trained over the pergola.

In Japan natural stone is used for stepping stones, usually in irregular shapes and chosen to blend with the local area.

A covered pergola   A plywood roof can be put over the posts and beams with roofing felt on top finished with a layer of grit. On top of that can be fixed the overhanging construction of bamboo canes and everything will look fine. You can fix bamboo canes on the underside or if need be rush matting, but that is less authentic.

A Japanese roof   In almost every garden in Japan there are archways or little roofs to shelter under from the rain or the sun. Little roofs are built particularly in front of entrances and the gateway will be under a small roof. They are usually made of wood, sometimes bamboo. The roof itself is usually made of wooden tiles which soon become green with a covering of moss. The guttering is bamboo, like the drain pipes. Sometimes dead leaves are deliberately left in the gutter so that ferns or other tough plants will soon grow there, and this gives a roof a weathered "old" look.

Left: In the mountains of Kyoto there are many temples for meditation. This is a courtyard with a well, covered against debris, and a water basin where you can scoop up water to rinse your hands and face.

In the Netherlands I have seen a little roof like the Japanese ones made with wooden roof tiles in a private garden. It looked beautiful.

Imagine this roof. There is a wall. In front of it is built a wooden terrace which overlooks a Japanese pool. Above that terrace there is the little pointed roof. The roof tiles are fixed on a framework of planks, the underside of which form the inside of the roof. It looks simple which is right for oriental – and especially Japanese – gardens and is appropriate for most patio gardens.

It pays to think hard about paving, as you can see from this design with various materials in a checkerboard pattern. Bricks and pebbles go well together.

A moss garden in the patio

My last Japanese idea for a patio is a moss garden. Now moss is a strange plant. If you want it, it is too dry, too sunny for it; if you don't, it grows freely among your plants and on the lawn.

There is something to learn from that. Moss grows mainly in closed, shady places, especially under trees. The water dripping from the trees in large drops makes a crust on the surface of the soil and there is no oxygen in the top layer. Moss has the chance to get established.

If you want moss, then the soil must be sandy – at least the top layer must – and you will need to scatter small pieces of moss on it. Over that spread weed-free river sand. Firm this a little and keep the moss damp. Keep it shaded as well. In the patio garden this can be done by closely planting the area where the moss grows with well-pruned *Acer palmatum*, the fine-leaved shrub maple, and *Prunus* with fine leaves and small pink flowers. Rake the leaves off the moss with a fine plastic

rake. If it succeeds, and it certainly will with sufficient shade and moisture, then you will have created something sophisticated in which a single stone is sufficient as a feature.

Alternatively, a number of clipped, round box or azaleas fit into this scene equally well, too.

I designed this water garden in a meadow in Axel. The meadow became a garden. The bridge is at a higher level and steps lead down. The view under the bridge gives an interesting effect.

Ornamental grasses, bamboos, and some ground cover

Ornamental grasses and bamboos still do

not receive the recognition they deserve.

Even in winter they remain attractive.

Festuca glauca is native to Western Europe, growing on sand dunes. It is low growing and drought resistant. The taller *Helictotrichon sempervirens* grows to 30 to 40cm (16 to 16in) and then has seed heads resembling wheat on long drooping stems. *Leymus arenarius* is also blue-grey. Its common name is lyme grass. It too can grow in dry places.

This is probably the most uncontrollable grass of the three. If you have a bed surrounded by slabs then it will soon be filled with a profusion of blue-grey stems. It is ideal for pots and containers.

Green ornamental grasses

There are many species and varieties of green ornamental grasses, tall or short, wispy or bushy. Sometimes they flower — but actually all grasses flower to produce seeds to reproduce. There are species with striking flowers and others with insignificant ones. *Stipa gigantea* is very striking, it can grow to 2m (6ft) high and it flowers with bronze-coloured spikes on strong stems which defy wind and rain. *Achnatherum (Stipa) calamagrostis* is fine though less bushy; it flowers from midsummer until late autumn with light, drooping ears. *Pennisetum compressum* is a green grass that forms a broad round clump which throws up unusual spikes in summer. They always remind me of hairy torches, which in this case are bent over gracefully. The grass is golden-yellow in winter. *Festuca*, fescue, is part of

*On the right is the purple loosestrife (*Lythrum salicaria), which is native to western Europe. Left at the back is yellow iris, with the golden variegated bamboo and a long-leafed variety in the foreground.*

85

our turf. *F. alpina* has very fine leaves. *F. gauteri* forms an evergreen clump, while *F. tenuifolia* is bright green and remains low growing.

Melica uniflora resembles quaking grass; the leaves are long and pointed. The grass is valued for the flowering stems on which the spikelets hang like drops of water. In the Thyssepark in Amstelveen, probably the most beautiful park in the Netherlands, a hill under beech trees has been planted with *Melica uniflora*.

The result is quite breathtaking. If you want an atmosphere of tranquillity on the patio, choose this grass and plant it in flowing shapes in gravel or between setts.

The grass I use the most belongs to the species *Miscanthus*. It is a variety which grows to a full height of 3m (10ft), *M. sinensis* 'Giganteus', which makes a tremendously strong vertical feature in a corner against a patio wall; it is a very sturdy plant. One problem is that it is difficult to control because of the tough root system. An axe is needed to get through it. A separate bed with a kerb is one solution. If there is room you can let it go. One tip: cut off the leaves as soon as the lowest ones turn yellow to prevent dead leaves blowing about. If *M.s.* 'Giganteus' reaches 3m (10ft), *M. sinensis* 'Silberfeder' is shorter and can produce lovely flower spikes. There is a silver

Beside pools there must be rounded shapes and only a few upright forms. Here are upright Butomus *(flowering rush),* Typha *along the edges, and* Scirpus *(rush), obtainable in many forms. Groups of* Pontederia *are rounded. Here they are in the foreground with other plants such as marsh marigold and flowering rush.*

streak in the leaf, hence the name, which means 'silver plume'. My favourite is *M. sinensis* 'Gracillimus', which has drooping leaves that grow on tall stems so that it forms a decorative clump under which other plants can grow. It is golden-yellow in the winter. *M. sinensis* 'Strictus' is upright and has yellow stripes. There is almost endless variety in this interesting species.

Yellow-leafed grasses

Cortaderia selloana 'Gold Band' is about 50cm (20in) tall and has long curving decorative leaves, which have yellow stripes on the outer edges. *Glyceria maxima* 'Variegata' has a yellow- and green-striped leaf.

Hakonechloa macra 'Aureola' has yellow, elongated, drooping leaves and is perfect combined with perennials in blue shades like *Salvia* and *Hosta*.

Milium effusum is a golden-yellow grass without stripes, at least if you choose the variety 'Aureum'. It has not very noticeable but quite attractive stems which are also light coloured.

Silver-striped grasses

Phalaris arundinacea has many white stripes on its elongated leaves – at least, the variety 'Feesey' does. It forms an attractive clump, while *Molinia caerulea* 'Variegata' fans out elegantly. Like

The magenta Geranium psilostemon *goes well with* Artemisia ludoviciana. *For even lower-growing ground cover in the same shades choose* Geranium sanguineum *and* Artemisia schmidtiana 'Nana'.

the golden variegated grasses, I rarely plant these silver grasses because they can soon make the planting look rather artificial.

There is also a silver variety in the indestructible *Miscanthus* family, *M. sinensis* 'Variegatus', which grows elegantly.

It reaches a height of 1.2m (4ft) and has long leaves, which are almost strap-like.

Using ornamental grasses   The forms that grow with graceful tall stems or attractive overhanging leaves can be planted among roses and perennials. A well-known combination is the blue *Helictotrichon sempervirens* between roses. I plant "my" *Miscanthus sinensis* 'Gracillimus' singly among low- and medium-growing perennials, and it is also useful between ground-cover plants such as *Pachysandra*, *Vinca*, and *Euonymus fortunei* 'Carrierei'.

Short ornamental grasses are best planted as single clumps among low perennials or as larger groups.

A patio with grasses only   Anyone who is interested in grasses can create something spectacular. There is first of all a normal lawn which is kept mown. Then a good "shape" must be built up with areas of low-growing grasses

Bonsai opens up an elegant world of gardening. Outdoor bonsai can be left outside in a cool place in winter, indoor bonsai must be kept indoors in winter. In summer both can be displayed on nice staging or tables.

and wedge-shaped groups of medium height behind. Right at the back come the tallest grasses. Choose *Luzula sylvatica* (woodrush) as an evergreen layer and tufted grasses with the clump-forming *Festuca gautieri* for evergreen areas.

You could perhaps plant some bamboo for winter interest.

Bamboo, an exotic plant
In Asia bamboo grows abundantly in the wild. This is a difficult plant to domesticate, which is however valued as food (bamboo shoots), building material (walls, beams, drain-pipes, and so on) and for fabrics and all kinds of cooking utensils. The plant itself is enormously variable. In general the leaves are usually elongated and the stems slender, but thicker bamboo stems do occur.

In northern Europe these thicker stems do not appear in the garden. The species here are confined to the hardy ones, which certainly limits the choice. My favourite varieties are those that have proved to be fairly hardy.

First there is *Sinarundinaria* (syn. *Fargesia*). This forms reliable clumps which can soon become quite broad, and it does not get out of hand. There are two species which are very similar. Both have light-green, decorative leaves. They are not fully hardy and in my

Ivy can be pruned to a low hedge over a frame of wire-netting, an earth bank, or sleepers.

89

exposed country garden they even become bare. In a sheltered patio garden they will keep half their leaves. The fresh green leaves sprout in May. Luckily they do not form rhizomes so they can safely be planted as specimens in the patio. *S. murielae* has pretty drooping stems, while *S. nitida* is more upright.

Phyllostachys is very invasive, but if anything even more beautiful. It is more upright and more branching lower down. There are both yellow- and black-stemmed varieties, *P. aurea* and *P. nigra* respectively. The rhizomes often grow underground for some way before they put up shoots; the plants are lovely in large patios but take up too much space.

I usually plant them in a plastic container with holes in the bottom. That limits their expansion.

Pleioblastus is the name for a large family of bamboos. There is a golden variegated variety which goes well with lady's mantle, the yellow *Sedum kamtschaticum* and *Hypericum*. At 1m (3ft) it makes a smaller feature. *P. variegatus* with a striking white-striped leaf is also low growing. *P. humilis pumilis* has green leaves and forms clumps up to 1m (3ft) high, *P. pygmmaeus* to 20cm (8in). *Pseudosasa japonica* is the bamboo with the longest history in our

Miscanthus sinensis *'Silberfeder' here forms a large clump which in spring produces elegant, silver plumes.*

Facing page: The ornamental Pennisetum alopecurioides *forms the round clump in the centre. It turns golden-yellow in autumn, then brown, and is cut down in spring. It produces lovely, purplish-brown plumes.*

parks and gardens. This is the plant that flowers once and then dies. It almost caused a disaster some years back in Burma because it seemed that the pandas were going to be deprived of their staple diet of young bamboo shoots. So the pandas were air-lifted by plane and helicopter to safer areas. It is not only in the inaccessible countries of Asia that *Pseudosasa* suddenly flowers. It happened suddenly simultaneously all over the world because bamboos have been planted in many gardens as a winter feature. This flowering seemed to signal the end of the plant and there has been a lot of damage caused in gardens where the bamboos have become indispensable evergreen thickets. So be warned, even though the experts may say that it only flowers once every eighty years. If they are right it is true that you can safely plant a healthy *Pseudosasa* to enjoy during your own lifetime.

Sasa veitchii reaches 1.2m (4ft) and has very broad leaves with a lighter edge. The green of the leaf fades so that the edge becomes rather shrivelled but it is still attractive. A problem with *Sasa* is that it spreads by underground shoots. So in the patio it is safer to give it an enclosed bed.

Using bamboo   In the gardens I design for modern buildings I try for the most part to fit in bamboo. If there is a blank garden or house wall then a

The water plants have upright forms to balance the horizontal water surface. Above, Scirpus *has brown flowers, while* Typha angustifolia *(bulrush), a cultivated form, is preferable to the taller wild* Typha latifolia *for a small garden.*

Upright grasses grow here in a horizontal mat of moss. There are many varieties of Stipa *and* Juncus *(rush) to use for these vertical lines.*

clump of bamboo placed against the wall and then repeated to left or right further forward is attractive. It gives depth. Bamboo is lovely by a window too; the view is beautifully framed by the overhanging branches. Bamboo is very suitable near water, particularly to emphasize the shape after the summer when the roses and perennials are past their best. If you like straight lines you can plant it in a row with or without interplanting; you can even make an angle, which reflects the lines of the house and the patio boundaries. You can really juggle with these lovely plants.

Plant the shorter varieties under a tree or under an upright shrub. If it becomes too crowded, thin out the bamboo. I often see bamboos that have been clipped into a rounded shape at the top, so that the height and spread are limited. Always prune the young soft shoots. A light, ornamental shape can be achieved by thinning out stems at ground level.

In Denmark I have often seen bamboo used as hedging, which can work well, especially with the *Sinarundinarias*; it is all a question of clipping.

I designed this town garden with large decks, steps, a pool, and luxuriant planting in which the narrow-leaved Sinarundinaria (Fargesia) murielae *has grown to a small wood.*

The cottage garden

The name says it all, the cottage garden, pinnacle of country gardening, the essence of the English gardening tradition. A cottage garden is ideal for the gardener who does not want to stick to detailed rules.

A cottage garden is not the same as a country garden and in the countryside we often see pleasant, old-fashioned plants and groupings that we no longer come across in sophisticated town and "executive" gardens.

Country gardens are often refuges for old-fashioned plants. The fact that the colours have not been thought out adds to their charm. In English cottage gardens there are unsophisticated combinations but often with more feel for colour. The difference reflects the people who live there. Cottages were the homes of farm workers, small traders, old couples, or single people. A cottage was ideal for them, not large but snug and easy to heat. Under a thatched roof they seemed especially comfortable. Today it is again often pensioners, single people, and small traders who live in them. Even richer people find these cottages more comfortable than a barn of a place which they can scarcely heat.

The small gardens are overflowing with left-overs and plants that have been there for many years. That is why in England people are so keen on these refuges for old-fashioned roses, perennials, annuals, and shrubs. Sometimes there is a vegetable patch, sometimes hollyhocks, phlox, and marguerites. If you are a romantic, then lay out a cottage garden like that in your patio. Remember that plants

New plants are constantly being added to the garden and borders, which I designed. They are examples of the elegant tradition of borders developed from country gardens.

The hydrangea was a real "cottage-garden" plant, at least until a few decades ago when it took over in ornamental gardens. This is Hydrangea macrophylla.

for a cottage garden are not chosen simply on the basis of colour. Keep some beds for vegetables and herbs, or plant a low hedge in front of the vegetable patch.

Anyone who thinks it odd to grow vegetables in a patio garden can grow hollyhocks, *Cosmos*, and sunflowers, or have a collection of roses – ones with lovely blooms – grown in rows purely for cutting. When I was young we had two rows of richly manured beds with roses and there was nothing nicer than to cut great bunches of them.

It is not a bad idea to make your patio garden a flower arranger's garden at the same time. If you choose plants to flower at different times then you will be able to enjoy flowers for longer in the house, even when a rainy season limits your enjoyment of them out of doors.

For example, you can begin with early-flowering bulbs and end with late dahlias.
There is a wide variety of flowering times among the perennials too, as there is with shrubs.

Be generous with your favourite colours along paths and paved terraces on the edge of the lawn. Fill the flower-beds and do not make them too elegant. Here are deep purple Phlox, Geranium psilostemon, *and* Erigeron 'Darkest of All', *surrounded by light-blue shades.*

95

Lovely polyantha roses

All these *remontant* or perpetual roses, descended from Chinese and floribunda roses, are well worth the effort.

Rosa 'Marie Pavié' is one of the loveliest white roses I know. The small leaves are somewhat curled, which makes it look plump and light. It is scented. *Rosa* 'Little White Pet', in French 'Félicité Perpetué', is a good climbing rose with creamy-white flowers. The scent is not very noticeable. *Rosa* 'Nathalie Nijpels' is suitable for ground cover in the enclosed garden. Plant it near a terrace and enjoy the clusters of fresh pink flowers.

I use *Rosa* 'The Fairy' a great deal. It is a mutation from the weeping rose 'Dorothy Perkins'. *Rosa* 'The Fairy' is pink, a dwarf cluster-flowered bush, with tiny flowers, and it is ideal for a sunny slope or beside lavender in the low-maintenance garden. It produces new shoots which flower above the old clusters, and it reaches 40cm (16in).

Another very special rose is *Rosa* 'Guinée', which has large maroon flowers that are very fragrant. In my experience it is one of the most strongly scented varieties. The centre of the flower is dark and velvety.

Rosa 'Viridiflora' is special and lovely among pale green shades for bouquets. It can be cut over a long time because it goes on flowering.

Rosa 'Yvonne Rabier' has creamy-white flowers in dense clusters.

In the open-air museum of the rose, L'Hay des Roses, near Paris, dark-green double arches have been made of iron and covered in dark-green mesh. These are ideal for roses. The tops are either square or rounded. The trellis in the background is wooden.

About hybrid tea roses

In the patio garden it is sometimes useful to have a few large blooms which stand out in the profusion of smaller flowers. The hybrid tea roses can do this. They were bred in England by crossing roses from China with other roses. The best known is 'Peace', which is famous all over the world. 'Peace' is a lovely name for a lovely rose. In Sir Winston Churchill's garden at Chartwell, a rose walk is lined with it. *Rosa* 'Apricot Nectar', which has apricot flowers, blooms over a long season. *Rosa* 'Dainty Bess', which is not suitable for shade but very delicate, is an open rose with red stamens in pale pink flowers. These are two more of the many delightful varieties.

Rosa 'Queen Margareth' is a new, pink rose which flowers freely. The equally popular white, *Rosa* 'Iceberg', flowers abundantly and seems to be disease-free. It flowers though until late autumn. You can prune it to a low or tall bush, and you can also obtain it as a standard, which gives a splendid flowering effect. It looks lovely in the patio with grey lavender and *Artemisia*. *Rosa* 'White Wings' has single flowers and dark purple stamens, and gives a very graceful effect. It is not suitable for difficult places. *Rosa* 'Swaney' is a Meiland rose, named after the famous rose breeder from Antibes. It is used widely and covers the ground completely. It grows to about 50cm (20in). If you like yellow, choose *Rosa* 'Mrs Oakley Fisher', an open yellow rose which flowers less heavily but is very elegant.

Iron or wooden posts or frames which are specially made must be strong enough to take the great weight of flowering climbing roses. Try to keep the young shoots of roses and cut out the old wood. In my garden I have Rosa 'Mozart' and Hosta sieboldiana, plus box bushes and hedges.

The Spanish monarchs own the huge summer residence in Aranjuez which has a sunny inner courtyard.

Rosa 'Ophelia' has pink flowers, light with a hint of yellow at the base. It grows to 70cm (28in).

If you buy a rose catalogue you will see that there are many more varieties to choose from. The ones mentioned are good varieties which are elegant and, in some instances, unusual.

Old walls are suitable, indeed ideal, for espalier shrubs and climbers. They hold the warmth and break the wind so that the climbers do not blow down.

David Austin roses

David Austin roses are remontant shrub roses in delicate colours. The English rose breeder David Austin names many of his roses after characters in *The Canterbury Tales*, or after people famous in gardening history such as Constance Spry. The roses have warm, delicate colours which are always elegant. They often flower repeatedly.

Previous page: Harold Acton, the famous writer, planted roses against his Florentine villa so that they continued the line of the windows and door frames. The Prussian blue of the paintwork is unusual.

Rosa 'Constance Spry' has large pink flowers with a lighter edge, blueish-pink is probably the best description. *Rosa* 'Chaucer' is similar to 'Constance Spry' but is perpetual. *Rosa* 'Wife of Bath' is also pink but with a deeper-coloured heart. *Rosa* 'Prioress' is pale apricot with a delicate open bloom, and is button-shaped in bud. *Rosa* 'Shropshire Lass' is also pale apricot, but shot through with pale pink. Graham Stuart Thomas is the man who helped David Austin in his search for new roses, in delicate shades, which are perpetual flowering – at least, almost all of them are. The rose named after Graham Stuart Thomas is butter-yellow. It grows to 1 to 2m (3 to 6ft).

100

Ornaments

Anyone who reads the gardening

magazines and garden

supplements knows how

much attention is being

paid to garden orna-

ments these days.

Containers, furniture, lighting; there is too

much to choose from in shops and garden

centres.

Ornaments are a very wide subject that can be interpreted in many different ways in the garden. The simplest is to try to create a lovely patio garden with as many plants, terraces, steps, pergolas and pools as possible. If you succeed, then ornaments are just necessary features to sit on or under. Another option is to make the most of containers and lovely container plants, designing your own compositions with plants and statues. Then the garden will become a gallery. A third option is to confine yourself to one element, for instance iron, and look for any objects made of iron that can be used as ornaments. There is a lot to be said for all these options so each will be looked at in turn.

Don't be in a hurry to throw away plants which have become too big. In a red terra cotta pot or an ornamental one they can become almost sculptural in form. They will need trimming.

Plants as ornaments

Anyone who is familiar with old gardens knows that the composition of trees, low green shrubs, low walls, and terraces with grass determines the composition. Ornaments are a sideline. Personally I try to achieve this effect in my gardens, but with one feature in the form of an ornament. It can be a statue or a bench; normally I aim to meet what has been agreed on the plans with the clients. Very often there are no ornaments at all, because the composition with the planting is attractive and interesting enough in itself. That is my ideal, that ornaments should not be necessary, but can be added to the garden if wanted.

If you have a patio and there is a long, interesting pool with a pair of grey shrubs behind it – together with a lot of *Hosta*, a species rose,

an ornamental tree with blossom and fruits, and, if possible, an angular hedge enclosing the pool – then the composition is balanced and complete.

Of course you want garden furniture, preferably chosen in a simple design in muted colours, made of either wood or iron. Anyone who does not like regular shapes will think of a patio filled with rounded features – not too many, perhaps three high ones on the back wall that you look across to and some lower round shapes by the terrace. Plant lavender, *Stachys*, *Nepeta* (catmint), and Christmas roses round them in long, flowing lines. If you like an oriental effect you must be very cautious about ornaments. Choose plants which achieve their form by being planted close together and then being clipped into rounded shapes on the top. This can be done with *Ilex crenata*, with Japanese azaleas, and with box. Plant simple shapes of periwinkle, ferns, *Pachysandra*, and *Skimmia* to achieve long, undulating shapes which are surrounded by gravel. The taller features can be bamboo, clipped *Pinus cembra*, and *Acer palmatum* – which must also be clipped.

Prunus can be used for free shapes. Here the main features are plants to which, if you wish, a single, modest, stone feature can be added. If you want tranquillity, plant a green hedge so that all

The transition from inside to outdoors can be managed in many ways. The African hemp with its large leaves catches the light and points the way outside.

the shades are green and you have a green wall behind you. You will see that you can work with plants in many different ways. If the garden is still new, place a few pots of box; if you dare wait until the specimen plants achieve their shape and if you have money to spare, plant some larger, more striking examples.

The well-filled garden gallery Collecting runs in the human race and has probably done so for centuries. Anyone who has seen the crowded Spanish patios with flower-filled pots everywhere, fountains, and glazed pots with azaleas knows that the tendency to give patios depth with the help of objects is almost universal. A patio may become an inner square with a tree here and there, some large groups of *Acanthus*, roses in pastel shades, and lavender. Anyone who can afford it can use stone in the form of an elegant fountain or spout, a lovely trough, a statue on a pedestal, or a carved fruit basket. Anyone who can't afford that will choose terra cotta which nowadays can be durable and of good quality. The cheaper products are inevitably less frost proof. The most expensive are lovely thick pots, sometimes plain, sometimes wreathed in garlands. Put round box bushes in them and save some for summer bedding plants. Vines and lilacs also do well in pots. Plant everything in black plastic inner pots and stand these in the terra cotta pots to prevent the pots from being shattered if the compost freezes.

This collection of pots with house plants is moved indoors for the winter. There is a successful contrast between their restraint and the luxuriant planting in the garden.

Grey wood is lovely for ornaments and furniture. It can be used for a feature such as a deck chair or as a seat for sitting and dining outside. Anyone who has had enough of terra cotta will look for alternatives. Galvanized iron buckets, watering cans, containers and pure ornaments are now plentiful; I have given in to them although I had resolved not to.

Antique seats are difficult to find and to transport. This example in stone with a lovely half-rounded back dates from the baroque era.

So now the huge, grey wooden table beside my farmhouse is piled with feed bins with handles, all with pots in them; there is a watering can with a long spout beside it and some other small items. The result is attractive, the cool grey of the zinc complements the warm grey of the wood. I intend to leave it at that until I come across something really special...

Concrete for ornaments

From way back nice benches have been made of concrete for use in the urban situation.

If you have a modern patio house, think about these simple benches without a back. They have long, flat seats and legs 40cm (16in) high, which are as broad as the seat. They can look very effective. Put them behind a pool in a line or on a cobbled terrace.

The present-day fashion for making compositions gives us the opportunity to experiment with combinations of objects and pot plants. The blanching pot (right) is put over vegetables which need to be white, not green. More lovely pots contain Hosta, *box, and low, creeping rock plants.*

In Amsterdam the gardens are often long and narrow because of the shape of the plots they are built on. In the long garden in the diagram I introduced divisions such as terraces, arches, and flowerbeds which stand out from the rest of the rather wild planting. What I found there was a garden gone wild, with even a smuggler's path. The arches are also used at point 9 to make a children's play area; swings were hung from them. The formal garden became a herb and a rose garden and received enough light to survive. The huge copper beech, which is far too big for a small garden, forms the core of the whole design and in the summer it becomes a deep red canopy which dominates everything. The lungwort, Christmas roses, and autumn anemones form a delicate counterpoise along the paths, where there is always something in flower.

Patios in Amsterdam

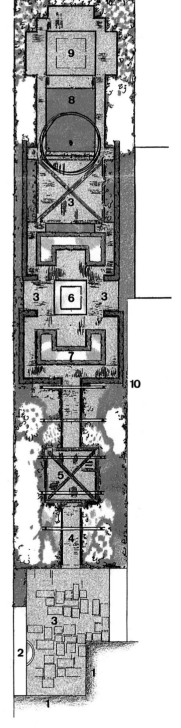

1 house, basement

2 fountain with spout against the wall

3 terrace near house

4 brick path with arches

5 brick terrace

6 pool with lead spout

7 beds with herbs and roses

8 ground cover suitable for deep
   shade, such as ferns, *Asperula*,
   and *Pulmonaria* 'Mrs Moon'

9 play area for the children, with
   swings attached to arches

Conservatories: extra room or paradise for plants

In England the conservatory has a long tradition and on the continent it is now catching on too. In essence it is a glasshouse, whether attached to the house or not, forming a light, sunny extension.

I find myself being asked more and more often by clients, sometimes with some prompting, to create a new living area by the house in which plants can be included. It always seems to be a success, provided a number of conditions are satisfied.

Firstly, different people want to enjoy the sun for different lengths of time. Secondly, people often want to sit and relax in the conservatory. Thirdly, they want accommodation for plants. The conservatory is then a room with plants and no longer, as originally conceived, a place to raise and grow unusual plants. Some people wanted to flower an orchid collection; others to protect their fuchsias and geraniums in winter; a third was crazy about ferns or palms, cacti, and little orange trees.

It only becomes apparent that different groups of plants have different requirements for humidity, temperature, and amount of sunshine when particular plants don't survive or can't be persuaded to flower. That was often a hard lesson, which led to people only putting the very toughest plants in the conservatory – a pity, because with a bit of forethought conditions could have been made suitable for the favourite plants which were often the reason for having the conservatory in the first place. The plants would have had a hundred per cent success rate.

This terrace with its flat roof enables many plants to be kept inside because of the protection given. The walls have been painted yellow, like the roof beams. Similar beams can be erected in a greenhouse with a pointed roof; that makes it cosy and trailing plants can grow in pots hanging from the beams.

Sun in the winter, shade in the summer

My assumption is that people as well as plants must be able to stay in the conservatory. That doesn't have to be all year round – for instance, not in winter and the height of summer. There are a number of plants that need reasonably cool conditions in the winter, like *Fuchsia*, passion flower, and citrus shrubs; they require a rest period. Then the conservatory must be kept cool, although a heating system keeps it frost-free. That is often not comfortable for people, although I do know some "die-hards" who will put on a thick jacket and enjoy the sun in the winter. Personally I am an outdoor freak who wants to enjoy every minute of winter sun from under the shelter of a covered terrace. I find the conservatory that can be open in winter ideal. The result is that orchids, palms, and tropical plants are not options for me. A greenhouse with ordinary glass would be sufficient, but then I have to do something about the summer temperature. A greenhouse of that kind reaches blood-heat in summer – far too hot to sit in. My solution is simple but effective; ensure that plants which are bare in winter shade the greenhouse in the summer and the problem is solved. Sometimes I plant grape-vines, which are trained over the roof, on the outside. They are bare in the winter but covered in foliage in the summer, and I can prune them more or less according to the amount of shade needed. That means that I have to use a ladder to reach the roof in summer. I can imagine that being a problem for some people. If

Pink and red geraniums, Pelargonium, *have made a fascinating wall here with* Fuchsias *hanging above them which have the same red in the tube of the flower. The Prussian blue ironwork is a good choice. Note that you can achieve maximum effect with simple, sturdy plants.*

you remove the plants from the greenhouse in summer then the vine can romp all over, unclipped, so that the roof is covered and from inside there is a green ceiling and the extra bonus of bunches of grapes. The vine does have to be pruned in winter. If you cannot do it yourself, ask a gardener or a friendly neighbour to help you. If you want to avoid pruning a vine, you could instead have standard trees in front of the conservatory, bare in winter but moderating the temperature with their foliage in summer. These could be ball acacias, pleached limes, or perhaps a nut tree. All fruit trees are suitable, especially the ones that have to be pruned, because you can then choose the shape of the crown to give the patch of shade you want.

It is lovely to see the blossom and then the green foliage with later fruit, so it is a good idea to use fruit trees such as apples, cherries, pears, quinces, almonds, plums, and peaches.

Extra thought given to elegant and yet austere details of the windows and glazing bars does wonders in this Art-Deco conservatory.

The conservatory on the east, west, and north

The sun rises in the east, first at a low angle then gradually higher. The breadth of the sun's rays is fairly concentrated, while the mid-day sun shines on a much broader area. In winter the sun only rises 18 per cent at noon, when it has already gone off the east side of the house. At midsummer the sun reaches an angle of 62° above the horizon, so its rays will reach the greenhouse.

The east-facing conservatory

In the east-facing greenhouse, therefore, you will have problems with the increasing warmth of the sun. You can cover the glass with screens – that is, on the inside of the greenhouse, or even better you can have screens on the outside which are let down automatically. When I was studying in Boskoop I worked in a tree nursery where wooden screens were always fixed on the greenhouses. They were made of thin wooden (hardwood) laths which were joined by rings. In winter they could be rolled up to the ridge of the roof, and then let down in summer. The sunlight was limited to strips, which gave a lovely effect. Screens made of nylon cloth or other synthetics give a uniform shade which is easy on the eye but looks dull. You often see blinds made of white or unbleached cloth, with rings attached so they can be pulled up or down ropes. This is beautiful too; it looks Mediterranean. Be careful not to get condensation marks on them; that limits their use where humidity is high. It is a pity that such a nice shade limits the type of plant. The advantage of interior blinds is, of course, that you don't need to go outside to adjust them.

The west-facing conservatory

The sunset is often beautiful. If you live in a town or look out on a small garden you will not see much of it from the greenhouse because in winter the sun is hidden behind trees, houses, or fences – a pity, because it is very colourful. What applies to the east-facing

People used to build matching conservatories onto houses. The owner of this one, an antique dealer, could not resist making the transition from treasures inside to those outside with a classical bust.

conservatory applies here: screen it from outside, plant trees in front, or train a vine over the roof.

The north-facing conservatory

A conservatory on the north receives hardly any warmth from the sun, which is an advantage sometimes because it does not need to be shaded in the summer and the view is therefore uncluttered. It can be advisable to use double glazing and to think carefully about heating, so that it can be pleasant to sit there at other times of the year than the summer. Some thought is necessary for the plants too, which must be chosen for a shaded situation. *Ficus, Fatsia, Philodendron*, and all ferns enjoy shade and in the summer fill up a cool conservatory-greenhouse beautifully.

Given the space, no-one will want to limit the height of palms, bananas, and orange trees. A fountain and several terraces outside this conservatory give the effect of an outdoor square.

On the right, rather hidden behind some shrubs, you can see a large, dark-green conservatory suitable for working, swimming, sport, or social functions (The Pulitzer Hotel, Amsterdam).

Provide good lighting in the greenhouse too; small spots and lamps will give the house plants extra light during the darker months. By using them you are adding what the sun would normally provide, the play of light through the leaves.

Dark colours hold the warmth, light colours reflect the warmth back. In positions on the north wall, shades such as ochre, blue, and ox-blood red are very practicable. In other situations light colours, white, pale yellow, and pale blue are good to keep the warmth at bay.

Ventilation

Every greenhouse must have ventilators

which can be opened

near the ridge of the roof

so that the rising warm

air can escape, and also

in the side walls,

preferably low down, to let in cool air.

If you are at home all day this system can be manually operated. If you are out at work, then you need an automatic system to open and close the ventilators according to the temperature in the greenhouse. Remember that on frosty days in winter the sun can drive up the temperature inside the greenhouse so that the ventilators open automatically, and let in frosty air which damages the plants. The system must take account of this. Even if you have a fully automatic system it is useful to have a few ventilators that can be manually operated. And of course there are summers when the doors can be open. Everyone who has house plants knows that there is moisture to consider as well as warmth. The moisture given off by the plants can be sufficient to mist up the windows. Besides, they take oxygen which people need out of the air. If there are a lot of plants in the greenhouse, the atmosphere can become stuffy, so that fresh oxygen must be added. Apart from windows that open, whether manually or automatically, there must also be ventilation panels, low down in the greenhouse. These can be horizontal or vertical louvres. Except in very cold weather the greenhouse should be ventilated daily. If when you are working in the greenhouse you dislike a draught, this can be done early in the day. A ventilator could be the answer. Do everything possible to minimize the loss of heat and moisture and to let in sufficient fresh air; then you will enjoy a fresh, pleasant atmosphere which will suit the plants too. Warm, moist air encourages

Narrow ventilators can be built into the peak of the roof to let out excessive heat. Vines against the glass or blinds, inside or outside, are less attractive.

111

pests and fungal infections which threaten the plants. Don't just examine the leaf of the plant to check for this, look underneath for pests; red spider mites for instance are almost invisible pests which suck the sap from the leaves so that the plant looks faded and will be in poor condition.

Heating the greenhouse

A temperature just above freezing is sufficient to overwinter plants. That is very different from what is needed in a conservatory which is a living area. The conservatory should always be separated from the adjoining rooms so that they do not need to have the same temperature and humidity. In the winter especially you may want the room cooler while the conservatory with its Mediterranean plants can be kept warmer. If you like tropical plants the temperature and humidity will have to be higher than you would want in the house. It is clear that there must always be a division between the two areas that can be shut.

Limit heat loss as far as possible

A conservatory loses a lot of heat through the large area of glass. Glass itself is a poor insulator; double or even triple glazing is preferable. There is also reflective glass which allows a view from inside but prevents people looking in. This is not attractive. Then there is tinted glass, clear from the inside but coloured when seen from outside. This is acceptable if it is brownish-grey and the paintwork is a lighter colour. Blue glass is not so nice, and has to be used very carefully with, for instance, a blue greenhouse-conservatory and a lot of grey-leafed plants and blue flowering plants round it. If the conservatory-greenhouse is to be integrated in the living area with a connection that nevertheless can be shut, then the heating system needs to be very good.

Under-floor heating

If the conservatory-greenhouse is yet to be built it is worth having a concrete floor laid with one or two gaps for large plants that have to be planted directly in the soil. Vines will need that. An insulating layer is laid over the concrete and then the heating pipes, and finally a wood or tile floor which is heated. This gives a pleasant, even warmth. Leave it on throughout the cold weather because the floor and air above it take hours to warm up from cold. Under-floor heating is pleasant to walk on. Pots can be placed on it too. Growth is stimulated by the bottom heat. Under-floor heating is ideal for raising annuals and starting cuttings of fuchsias and geraniums. One advantage is that this system is not visible and it takes up no space. There are systems in which solar panels on the roof provide the heating, which is led under the floor.

Under-floor heating with solar panels

Energy saving is being encouraged and even subsidized nowadays. That is sensible because the warmth from the sun's rays can be easily collected in so-called solar panels. Water is fed through pipes

Facing page:
In warm weather the door is left open and the ventilators can be opened by an automatic system, which is activated as the temperature rises.

in the panels. The panels can be set in the garden, at an angle of 15 to 45˚. Alternatively the panels can be hidden behind a hedge in the vegetable garden or on the roof of the house or a shed by the house. The heat can then be led through pipes to the cellar where it is stored in a tank and distributed to the under-floor heating in the conservatory or living room. The cooled water is pumped back to the solar panels.

This wood and iron greenhouse is ventilated by opening panels in the sloping roof.

Radiators   Many greenhouses have radiators or heating pipes. If your conservatory-greenhouse is built on a wall, 40cm (16in) high, a radiator can be set against it, with an open-work cover above it. Pots with plants can be stood on it, or you can put cushions there to sit on. If the glass extends to ground level, pipes which run horizontally are advisable. Paint them green so they blend in, and stand plants in front of them. You can look out over them so they are not a problem. I recently designed a greenhouse in which the radiators were 15cm (6in) high, with a smooth outer wall, and open at the top. They looked like little walls. This system is expensive to install, but looks nice in the greenhouse because the radiators can be hidden behind plants and dark-green, black or grey paint helps to disguise them. There are many systems on the market which are used by experienced builders. Ask for their advice and think carefully about what type of plants you want in the conservatory-greenhouse. If you want a huge *Ficus benjamina* you have plenty of latitude; for orchids the atmosphere must be more humid; for cacti it must be drier; while tropical plants need warm, moist conditions. If you intend to keep books and other items that are affected by damp in the conservatory you will need to limit yourself to plants that like less humid conditions.

A lovely example   I once came across a modern house which had a small, narrow front garden, even less garden at the side, and a wide back garden, also small. Behind it was a strip of trees such as elm, ash, and alder bordering a busy road, so that the back garden was never used. The owners used to sit at the side of the house, behind a projecting wing, which reduced the traffic noise. I suggested building a brick wall 2.5m (8ft) high on both sides and at the back. In the back wall I left a gap in which a greenhouse was erected that reduced the noise of traffic. This was a success, and the back garden became the most popular place to sit. Water circulates through two pools over a waterfall and the sound blots out the rest of the traffic noise. The owner plays soft music in the greenhouse, which gives a pleasant atmosphere.

I do favour having a free-standing greenhouse elsewhere in the garden, instead of adjoining the house, since I believe the conservatory-greenhouse makes a splendid new space in which to potter about.

Workbenches are built round the walls in this greenhouse. To make it look less functional add a seat at the end and a small pool in the middle.

Rooms behind an integral conservatory tend to be darker and they are often downgraded to "evening" rooms. Besides, people walk to free-standing ones, whether or not under a covered verandah, and gain a different view of the house and garden. This also solves the problem of temperature in the greenhouse since it is not connected to the house. To be fair, it might be used less as a sitting area because the approach is in the open air. Clients with conservatory-greenhouses like this use them as sitting areas throughout the year except for a very short time. In any case you will often have to wear a jersey out there when the door is open.

In the greenhouse in the gap in the wall I laid a brick terrace in the middle. This linked up with the entrance in the side wall. To left and right there were wide containers for orange trees, *Agapanthus*, *Nerium* (oleander), *Plumbago*, ferns, and a single bonsai on a pedestal. A large stone table came to no harm when the greenhouse was being watered, nor did the cane furniture. It made a wonderful place. Heating was provided by low radiators which were unobtrusive because they were painted dark green to match the aluminium frame of the greenhouse.

Apart from the heating systems already mentioned there are of course electric heaters which work well. Work out how often you

Shelves can be used to display orchids. Here they form a cascade of flowers. A coat of whitewash on the outside will provide shade.

will need to use heating. A simple heater may well be sufficient and even with the relatively high electricity bills it could work out cheaper than installing under-floor heating or radiators. If, however, you do want to be able to sit in the conservatory at room temperature more or less the whole year round, then you will need to install a more elaborate system.

Almost the most photographed vegetable gardens must be Rosemary Verey's. At Château Villandry on the French Loire river there are further treats for photographers. This is an arbour about to be covered completely with golden hop, Humulus lupus.

Moisture, an essential element

It can be a problem in the conservatory to have to supply moisture to the plants which can then spoil books and furniture. This is not an insoluble problem because, for instance, there is furniture which can stand damp.

When the variegated ivy has grown all round this ornament it will give the necessary depth. The ram's head forms the spout.

But if you do paperwork in the conservatory you will have to be especially careful, have a lot of thirsty plants, and install very good ventilation to get rid of the moisture. Take care in your choice of material for cushions and curtains because not all fabrics are damp-proof by any means. The best solution is venetian blinds with narrow wooden slats, because they are rot-proof, like cane floor covering. Carpeting will not survive the damp. Rush matting, however, is suitable. In the higher humidity which is necessary for tropical and sub-tropical plants, appropriate materials will have to be chosen and the use of the space will have to be adapted to the conditions. Otherwise plants will have to be restricted to those that will survive in warm, dry air. Fortunately there are enough of these to create luxuriant surroundings.

Plants need water, but the amount varies according to the group they belong to. Think about their native area or look up their requirements in a book. Cacti like dry, warm air so they are ideal for the office-conservatory. *Geranium*, *Nerium* (oleander), *Fuchsia*, *Begonia*, and really all Mediterranean plants are happy in warm dry air if the soil is watered occasionally. As the air can be fairly dry, these plants are ideal for the conservatory-living room. Begonias do not really belong here, but they do extremely well in a dry atmosphere, provided the soil is moist. *Abutilon* can also stand a dry

atmosphere if the soil is damp. All plants from the rain forest, such as *Philodendron* and orchids, like a moist atmosphere and damp compost and they are thus suitable for the hothouse that has iron or rattan furniture.

You can use fountains, spouts, or jets of water to raise the humidity. Here the jets come from huge carved stone frogs.

How to water

Some conservatory owners swear by the spray on the garden hose to water the plants very gently. Some plants, orchids for instance, do not like being kept wet so much as having a moist atmosphere in which leaves and flowers thrive. Their roots do not need to be in compost but can attach themselves to something rough, the bark of a tree or the inside of a coconut, and draw moisture out of the air. They are unsuitable for a dry atmosphere. It makes a difference to moisture whether it is the cooler winter or the warmer summer that is being discussed. Plants need more moisture in summer, as they do in a heated conservatory in the winter. Remember this and give the plants more moisture in warmer periods.

The humidity can be raised by standing the plants on pebbles or a brick in their saucers, which are then filled with water that can evaporate. If you like pretty stones you can put them in the saucers round the pots. They do, however, become covered in green slime. If you want an easy life or are short of time you can install an automatic watering system. This can be a long hose with branches made

119

of thinner pipe. The system can be activated by a time-clock or a hygrometer. Ask at a good garden centre; there are all kinds of system on the market.

Anyone with the time will enjoy watering the plants with hose, spray, and watering can. If you need to water the plants frequently a tile floor is essential.

What sort of water? In general rain water is best for plants under glass because it is softer than tap water. By old greenhouses you will often come across a water butt where the watering can is filled up. Water is led off the roof. In old buildings there are commonly enormous cisterns under the gardens and houses for the same reason. If there is no room for a cistern like that then you can arrange for something to catch the water. A round drain pipe and a concrete floor with a water butt, or an attractive stone trough, can be placed under the water outlet to collect the water. Of course, the water must be at room temperature for the plants, which calls for an underground reservoir – and that will save space in the greenhouse. The alternative is to use tap water for the compost, the saucers, and spraying the leaves of the plants. Check whether the plants need any extra fertilizer which you can apply with the watering can.

A tap over an old stone sink makes a very attractive feature for watering plants. The vines are trained along wire. They are dusted with sulphur against mildew. Any water spilt helps to raise the humidity, which must not fall too low except for cacti and succulents.

Anyone with a creative bent will soon conjure up a small pool with

These galvanized watering cans are being made again. They are nicer than brightly coloured plastic ones. Collect them, then fill them with water so that it can warm up for watering the conservatory plants in winter.

goldfish out of a water reservoir and surround it with ferns. In romantic Victorian conservatories you often see water which circulates via a small pump and a length of hose cascading over boulders. This is an interesting feature because it increases the humidity of the atmosphere as well as looking pretty. If you want to translate this into the modern idiom you can make use of small round concrete slabs. In the Japanese style a stone is hollowed out and water drips into it from a bamboo pipe. The water is collected in a basin underneath and can then circulate. The fine stream of water gives a tranquil atmosphere and raises the humidity. I have often had something austere carved out of stone or assembled for water ornaments in the conservatory. Remember that all kinds of ferns love porous wet stones and will seed everywhere, which can be very attractive. Think about having the water running over or seeping out of tufa.

At one time a pump like this would have supplied water from the rain water cisterns for the greenhouse. Now we just turn on the tap, but rain water is still preferable.

121

The ambience in the conservatory

A "good" conservatory must be a restful place where it is pleasant, for instance, to sit and read. Plants and furniture, chosen to reflect personal tastes, contribute to this.

I am myself very fond of the Thai rattan-cane furniture with lovely big cushions. Some people will want to use the conservatory for reading and writing, drinking tea, and dining. This will influence their choice of furnishings.

I designed a garden in Sambeek to include a huge conservatory which houses a display of furniture suitable for the conservatory. There is a great range of items for sale. They include large natural stone tables on wrought- or cast-iron bases, plain or curved. Italian wrought-iron items with plaited iron strips for seats and backs, and copper studs on the back, are displayed. There is a huge selection of bamboo cane and rattan cane, together with hardwood in all kinds of shapes. Sofas, dining tables, chairs, and benches with or without cushions, according to your taste, are there too. Many garden centres have their own wide selection.

Wood is popular because of the lovely grey colour it develops if it is untreated. It can also be oiled and then a warm colour develops which goes well with white or cream linen cushions. Blinds of the same material, with rings on cord, or curtains for cold winter evenings will complete the decor.

This is a Victorian garden in a conservatory, complete with lovely flower beds, and paths with gravel and chippings, not forgetting the flowering shrubs. It is easy to keep this profusion at its peak for months.

Cane for eastern elegance

Rattan-cane furniture from Thailand has a classical elegance that gives a pleasant effect. It has a warm, light-golden colour which suits cushions in cream or pale fawn. The seat is plaited and the chairs stand on sturdy legs. The furniture can be used on the terrace or indoors in the dining room.

I recently designed a conservatory with interesting furniture. The sitting area is 3 x 3m (10 x 10ft); on either side there are larger closed-off sections for orchids and other plants in pots. There is a large grass-green Victorian rattan-cane sofa, two simple cane chairs with round backs, and a square Japanese cane table. The sitting area is lit by small spots. There is music and a telephone. A passion flower is growing along the roof and the sides are filled with flowering plants. Outside there is the knot garden. I have surrounded the beds with box edging and then planted flowers for cutting, such as *Delphinium, Thalictrum, Phlox, Alstroemeria,* and *Lysimachia ephemerum.* The conservatory is the last stage of the garden and could only be built when a large cedar had blown down. It is 13m (43ft) long, 3m (10ft) wide, and the height varies. There is a higher section in the centre. It was all built in standard sections to keep the cost down. There are two pipes under the panes for heating. For shading there are cloth blinds under the roof and along the side walls which are adjusted manually. In both conservatories there is a

I usually have my conservatories sprayed green but I left the bare aluminium in this case because with the profusion of green bay trees it gives a light and pleasant impression. We are now looking for a sociable atmosphere in the conservatory, a sort of symbiosis with the plants.

123

workbench at the back; the sitting area is in the centre. In the winter all the box topiary and other tender plants are housed there. In summer there are pots of scented climbing jasmine and a lot of blue *Plumbago* in pots. The conservatory has been fairly simply furnished because of the sea of colour in the garden outside. The nice thing is that it has made a new feature in the garden, where people can walk round, have a drink, and then move on. Here too it is separate from the house.

***Iron furniture,
decorative
open-work***

Iron is a good idea for chairs and tables in a small greenhouse or conservatory. Its open-work construction allows a view of the plants or the garden outside. If you want low maintenance choose a table with a stone top; iron quickly rusts in a damp atmosphere and needs frequent painting. And yet...rust is "in" and a rusting table with African violets and a hurricane lamp makes a romantic feature that costs very little.

There is more iron furniture apart from the chairs and tables, some with natural stone, lead, or hardwood tops. For example shelves – they can be semi-circular or straight – which offer several levels for displaying plants are very practical. A rack with cuttings and fuchsias in flower, with good varieties of geraniums, *Saintpaulias*, and *Streptocarpus*, can be beautiful if carefully thought out. There is

*Fortunately these
seats can now be
obtained in
aluminium, which
saves spending
hundreds of pounds in
an antique shop on
wrought-iron ones.
The effect is identical
when moss and
climbers have grown
round them.*

124

This long garden in Amsterdam has a mirror at the end of it, to make it look larger. There are begonias in hanging baskets in the conservatory.

also the "waterfall" feature with similar shades and leaf shapes. If you like variety you can really enjoy yourself with shelves. You can move plants into a prominent position as they flower and hide the ones that are over. There are very high sets of shelves available. The big wooden ones are not generally available any more; they were made of wood that had been treated and stained. A disadvantage of this construction is that it looks clumsy and takes up a lot of space so that a large greenhouse is needed with a blank wall to stand the shelves against. If there is glass on three sides of the conservatory the shelves can occupy the other wall, or they can be placed on either side of the entrance to the living room. If there is no blank wall, then use long, low shelves or make an island feature with two semi-circular stands.

If you see the conservatory primarily as a place to work and eat and you are less interested in growing special plants, then you will have to have a drier atmosphere, which limits the choice of plants. In that case there is no question of a large orchid collection, but there are *Saintpaulias, Streptocarpus, Geranium*, and *Fuchsia*. In a living area there is no workbench for potting but there can be shelves and attractive hardwood or stone tables at various heights. The floor can consist of terra cotta paving or grey, natural-stone slabs which do not show the dirt or damp.

In the reign of Queen Victoria everyone wanted to grow plants from South America, Mexico and South Africa. Pelargoniums (geraniums) were among the discoveries. Palms, pomegranates, tree ferns, oranges, and huge bay trees were kept in conservatories like this one, which is now empty. I would love to get to work here with pots and plants.

***A layout with
natural stone***

There are many good stone table tops available which are ideal for the conservatory. They are indestructible and they can be mounted on different bases. You can set them on pillars of dark-grey concrete or stone, or use a bistro design of black or dark-green iron. For dining tables there is a choice of round, square, or rectangular stone tops on wooden or wrought-iron bases, plain or curly.

Stone is good for the floor too. There are new slabs available in standard sizes of 20 x 40cm (8 x 16in) and square slabs 40 x 40cm (16 x 16in). If you like old materials, look for slabs which vary in colour because that is more attractive than the rather dull uniformity of grey slabs. With grey as a background, interest can always be added with lots of terra cotta pots or white earthenware and cane furniture in warm colours. I like plain floors. Cane furniture and baskets soon provide the desired warm effect. On the other hand, if the surroundings are too "warm" they can soon become fussy through the wrong choice of plants, even with just one pot of *Strelitzia*, the bird-of-paradise flower. A plain background is always advisable with this flower. The choice does depend on whether the conservatory faces south or north.

***Furnishings and
aspect***

A conservatory facing north will get very little sun except very early and late in the day provided there are no walls or trees to shade it.

Rosemary Verey has designed this new shelter, which is attached to her house, Barnsley Manor in Gloucestershire, very tastefully. The mood is set with sandstone pillars, green doors, and old sandstone slabs. Inside there is a waterfall and many house plants.

126

Light colours are best here. Terra cotta, red or light-red tiles, a lot of wood, and light-painted pots and shelves are used to liven up the decor. Pale-green or grey-green furniture is attractive, or blue furniture to contrast with the greenery. Then there can be patterned curtains and brighter blue, yellow, or white blinds. A conservatory facing south needs to be restful, therefore cooler colours are appropriate: terra cotta, grey, and dark blue.

A conservatory on the east or west can have something of both depending on how crowded it is with plants and furniture. In general, light furnishings are advisable in a west- or east-facing conservatory, because for most of the day – and just when people are sitting in there drinking tea or coffee or having a meal – the place is in shadow. That means having either a wooden floor or small red or light-red floor tiles, wooden tables, a lot of cane, and white or cream curtains and blinds. Yellow can be used too. Blue is rather cool, but all the shades of brick-red are good, although in the shade they sometimes show up as dark patches. Choose plants with pale leaves such as African hemp, grapevine, and ferns grown as standards so that the light shines down through the leaves.

Hanging baskets In a rather shady conservatory you must be careful not to take away too much light with hanging baskets. Yet a single basket with a

This was a complete design with white roses and perennials in a back garden in Axel. Originally there was a large central area with the same white shades but because the client found that too monotonous I put in a pond with a stone edging and two stone circles as water features.

pale-leafed ivy, white or pale-pink fuchsia, or the white-striped *Chlorophytum* can liven up a rather dull conservatory on the north, east, or west. In conservatories with a southern aspect baskets can provide dappled shade. Line the basket with plastic to prevent water dripping on to furniture, curtains, or wooden floors. A layer of *Sphagnum* moss can be laid in the basket under the plastic to hide it. Water the baskets carefully because plants do not appreciate sitting in waterlogged compost. If you have a stone floor and water splashes are not a problem you can omit the plastic. A great advantage of hanging baskets is that you can keep your plant collection in the roof.

A conservatory with hanging baskets

It is not easy to make something of narrow gardens, especially when tree-lined, because they all too often become a long, narrow room. This was not the case in one particular garden with plenty of seats, which was furnished as a sitting area and a paradise for plants. There was a central path and the garden was on different levels, with steps, which were used to make terraces. At the far end the garden widened out, giving space for sun-lovers such as herbs, roses, and perennials. In the continuation of the path there is a green-painted conservatory. A mirror has been fixed to the back wall which makes the conservatory itself appear much deeper – and indeed the whole garden. Baskets filled with large-leafed begonias

This enormous orangery is built of grey stone. The contrast between the sombre hard exterior and the delicate soft interior can be very exciting. When the doors are opened there are the sweet scents of lemon, Stephanotus, orange, and lily of the valley.

hang from chains in front of the mirror. These make the mirror much less obvious, which adds to the air of mystery. A world of illusion and fantasy could well be created in your own situation.

After all, people are eager to learn; you don't need to copy something exactly but you can learn from other people's ideas.

You can have a trial run with a cold-frame before you decide on a greenhouse. Plants can be raised or over-wintered in it.

Incorporating the conservatory

It is very important that the conservatory blends in with the garden. If it adjoins the house there are two possibilities. A terrace with pots can provide the transition from the conservatory to the garden.

Such a terrace can look cluttered and untidy, but the smooth transition is important. A large white parasol on the terrace will help to lower the temperature in the conservatory. It looks lovely if you use the same terra cotta pots, indoors filled with large *Abutilon* and outdoors with *Geranium* in the same colour.

The second possibility is to look for a contrast by surrounding the conservatory, with its wooden or stone floor, with luxuriant vegetation. Just imagine it: a pool near the conservatory with marginal plants reflected in the water. Use large-leafed kinds such as *Gunnera* which grows to a considerable height. This makes the conservatory look like a fairy-tale world.

The terrace is then deliberately extended further into the garden to create another distinctive area. Plant bamboo or ornamental grass, *Miscanthus sinensis* 'Giganteus', between the conservatory and the outdoor terrace. That creates an atmosphere of surprise and excitement; the conservatory will resemble a jungle. If you choose a tall bamboo then you will also be able to enjoy the tall clump in winter.

A formal external layout Frames which were protected by glass in the winter used to be placed in front of the winter gardens, allowing plants to be raised in them or over-wintered. The frames were sometimes heated. Usually

This greenhouse has been given an old-fashioned appearance, to blend in with its surroundings.

they were not. This idea of straight lines is shown very well in the greenhouse illustrated on page 130. It was built on an island which was turned in to a garden. The rectangular island has been divided up by grass paths, bordered by hedges, which divide up the garden into four garden rooms. One of these has become a nursery with an old-fashioned greenhouse in it.

This was built from demolition material by Mr Canneman, who as architect with the National Commission for Historic Buildings had access to old materials. Small windows were put in and the wood-work was painted white. Pillars of old bricks were built against the side walls as load-bearing structures, between which the wooden window frames were fixed. This gave it a romantic look which is absent from many modern greenhouses.

The garden in front of the conservatory

Looking from the greenhouse towards the surrounding hedge you see to left and right a pair of nursery beds in which delicate plants were nurtured. For example, lily of the valley and miniature cyclamen were forced, together with an endless series of bulbs and tubers. These were in flower much earlier because they had been grown in these cold frames rather than out in the open. Pot plants from the south, too, were over-wintered here, such as *Ballota*, while some fuchsias survived in the frame. To the left there is a large bed with hollyhocks, rocket, *Geranium*, Mediterranean jasmine trained

The patio garden does not need to be without green even if you do not like mowing grass. Plants in all kinds of pots and containers can be combined with climbing plants on the walls to give plenty of green.

up canes, and oleanders which are placed outside during the summer. It is a treat to be in this particular garden.

What you can learn from the greenhouse I have described is that brick with glass and wood makes a good romantic combination. If you actually want to raise plants then a workbench is handy. If there is a brick wall behind the bench pots can be stored under it. The work surface stands on brick pillars. The roof projects over it. On the inside of the greenhouse there is a *Hoya* – wax plant – and a *Stephanotis* which is beautifully scented.

In winter it is full of cuttings and also the orangery plants overwinter here in their tubs.

The second lesson is that it is a good idea to give a greenhouse like this a "nursery" character by having terraces with containers and pots in front of it. That also makes it easier to bring plants indoors for the winter.

Formal beds with box edging — If you like a formal style you can lay out a garden in front of the conservatory with square beds on either side of the path that leads to it. You can plant these up to suit your taste. There can be a place for *Datura*, *Abutilon*, and *Nerium* in pots sunk in the ground. There can be annuals, or perennials, herbs and roses as well.

The chimney shows that this greenhouse can be heated. It provides winter accommodation for treasures such as bay trees, citrus shrubs, oleanders, palm, pomegranates, and myrrh. Add a little lane with pears trained over an arch, or a wall with espalier pears and a bench to relax in the shelter of the wall.

It is a good idea to introduce some fixed elements since this can look very bare in winter. Box edging is evergreen and gives shape to the whole. You can also plant clipped box bushes in the beds.

Uniformity in box beds

To be very daring choose one plant for the beds, preferably in a different green from the box. Choose rosemary, the silver-grey *Santolina*, or lavender with purple flowers. *Santolina* has yellow or pale lemon-yellow flowers, depending on the variety. Variegated *Salvia purpurea* is nice too, like gold- or silver-variegated sage, mint, and so on.

If you find this too flat, put in a row of standard roses which reflect the colour of the planting in the conservatory.

If you have white cushions and blinds in the conservatory, then plant the white standard *Rosa* 'Marie Pavié'; if the interior decor is yellow, then choose *Rosa* 'Peace' as a standard outside; and if the interior is pink, try *Rosa* 'Bonica', which blooms for a long time. In this way you can create unity between conservatory and garden.

Necessary camouflage

I once saw a very good adaptation of a newly built greenhouse. It was a standard, wooden model that did not fit in with the local rustic style. Fortunately the owner had laid out the surrounding area

If the plants are the most important feature the greenhouse must be inconspicuous, for example a reflection of aluminium and glass.

133

to give it a completely different character. There were wide beds separated by grass paths. The beds were planted with annuals and biennials such as hollyhocks, mullein (*Verbascum thapsus*), dill, fennel, and the cardoon (*Cynara*). There was a sea of grey, green, and colour round the greenhouse which camouflaged the newness of the building. Of course in the winter it looked bare, so it was suggested that shrubs were planted for winter interest, either evergreens or ones with interesting shapes.

A *Viburnum x burkwoodii* remains grey-green, like the *Eleagnus*, and has lovely scented flowers. Prune these shrubs regularly to keep their shape. *Eleagnus* in particular will otherwise get out of hand.

You can plant hedges round the greenhouse. If there is no space for a separate garden then plant a beech or hornbeam or if need be a yew hedge. If the greenhouse is to be visible in winter then use deciduous trees such as larch so that the sun can warm the greenhouse during the winter. Do not plant the hedge too close unless you want a cooler greenhouse.

Facing page: In England conservatories with the romantic look have been popular for a long time. They give an impression of comfort and relaxation. You can fill them with plants too.

The setting

I have already talked about planting

deciduous trees near the

conservatory to provide

summer shade. Fruit

trees are ideal for this.

You have to prune these trees, which means you can tailor their shape to provide the shade needed. If the greenhouse is on the north, east, or west, it is more a question of not spoiling the view from the terrace or the garden. That can be done with fruit trees if they are not too thick. There must still be plenty of light in the greenhouse, so plant the trees further away or choose less dense, small ones.

Arches have been used from way back for training pear trees. This oak arch looks authentic.

Climbers for the conservatory

If you drive through the market-garden area in Belgium south of Brussels, you see many greenhouses with vines which have been planted outside but then led inside. The roots of the vine are not confined by the base of the building. The fruiting branches grow indoors, which means an early crop. Grape-vines need winter rest and only grow if the greenhouse is barely heated. They are therefore not suitable for the conservatory which is lived in. There are other possibilities of course.

Climbers on the outside

If you like a cool greenhouse in the summer you can train a grape-vine over the roof outside. It will have to be pruned in winter, which is a nuisance but it can be done. Prune in summer to remove all the shoots above the vine in order to speed up ripening of the grapes which will receive most of the nourishment from the roots. Otherwise it is wasted on lengths of trailing stems.

Here there are many walls. I used box edging for the flower-beds and then yew to make a low screen in front of the wall. People are fascinated by the green wall of espalier pears and do not notice the brick wall so much.

If you only want foliage, summer pruning is not necessary and you can enjoy the sunlight filtered through the leaves as you sit inside. The same can be done with *Wisteria*, roses, *Aristolochia* (birthwort), and many other plants. If your greenhouse is on the north then plant honeysuckle, for instance *Lonicera periclymenum* 'Serotina', which smells lovely and provides shade. Kiwi provides good camouflage too. The large leaves and luxuriant growth make the shape of the greenhouse inconspicuous.

It may be sensible to paint a rather ugly white structure green. British racing green is a good colour, or dark blue and black, or simply pale colours. With a hardwood greenhouse avoid using oil or varnish and let it weather to grey, then the shape is less obvious. Aluminium structures can be sprayed to your taste beforehand. Let someone else do it and spend your time on your plants.

It is odd that decrepit old fruit trees are more attractive than the neat, upright ones we grow ourselves. This is a lovely example.

Construction materials

Nowadays there is no end of materials available. You could be inspired by old examples or choose something ultra-modern.

The earliest orangeries were brick built, with or without a layer of plaster. You saw how bricks formed the basis of the structure at Walenburg Castle with the windows between them and the roof supported by them. The look of the old bricks makes it an idea worth copying.

Apart from using brick, with wood for the window frames and roof, there are also all-wood greenhouses available. These are usually made of cedar to resist rot, which can attack painted or untreated softwood. If you want a very dry greenhouse you can use treated pine. Keep the painting or staining up to date because you never know if there is a less-resistant piece in the structure. Apart from hardwood that you can allow to bleach, or that can be painted (preferably not white!), there is also iron.

Iron structures   Many older types of greenhouse are made of narrow iron straps and beams. The disadvantage is that the metal was not galvanized and there will be rust in the corners because of the moisture. Swelling will have followed, which shattered the glass. If you do have an old greenhouse like this you know what will happen if you do not have it well restored. It will cost a lot of time and effort. Yet these structures have a certain charm. Consider whether to paint it or dismantle it and have it galvanized and then rebuild it. The latter is the

The covered terrace under the pointed roof has wooden seats, painted black to match the plant containers.

When I designed this roof garden my starting point was black and white for floor and seats. It is a lovely extension which can be used for the whole year.

best plan. An alternative to iron has now been found, namely rust-proof aluminium.

I almost always have it sprayed before assembly, preferably dark green or dark blue, because aluminium is not particularly attractive. Clearly with a conservatory adjoining the house you must look carefully at the transition; either use a contrast or keep the same style for the conservatory as the house. Wood often seems to provide the best combination, especially with older houses. Aluminium provides a contrast which can be attractive if the design is good.

However, one often sees very ugly imitation conservatories which simply do not go with the house. A construction like that will reduce the value of your house. It always pays to spend money on a good design.

From conservatory to terrace

When I came across a rusty iron greenhouse in Haarlem I decided to take out the glass and build a new one in the sun. That stands east–west with the highest part on the south, unlike the old one which stood on the north side, half in shadow. The old structure was covered with climbing roses, clematis, and honeysuckle. It made a shaded terrace for meals and drinks. When the new greenhouse is built it will take over as a paradise for plants.

The profusion of plants in containers gives the impression of a more rural situation than the surroundings would suggest. Evergreens provide year-round interest.

139

A few easy-to-grow plants for effect

Abutilon comes in various heights and there are variegated varieties. *Abutilon pictum* 'Thompsonii' will grow in the conservatory, can be pruned when necessary, and makes a striking feature. There are small-leafed species, *A. megapotamicum*, including a variegated cultivar, *A.m.* 'Variegatum' with finer, narrower leaves and a yellow flower. It needs a minimum of 1– 4°C.

Acacia (mimosa) becomes a tough shrub in the conservatory and apart from its fine leaves it has fluffy yellow flowers, which are great favourites.

A. dealbata flowers when young, while *A. retinoides* 'Lisette' flowers throughout the winter with pale-yellow scented blossoms. It needs a minimum temperature of 4 –5°C.

Ardisia is a shrub with long, evergreen leaves. Bunches of red berries follow the fragrant white flowers. It is frequently offered as a standard.

Bambusa can reach 2.5m (7.5ft). This invasive plant is safe grown in a pot or a separate bed with a concrete surround. It has fine, evergreen leaves. Minimum temperature 0 –7°C.

This house near Antwerp has a swimming pool in a white aluminium conservatory. In front of it there is a wooden deck for sun-bathing with minimalist green features such as the box ball.

This free-standing, hardwood conservatory provides space for relaxing with tea and a book. The plants are for decoration until the winter, when tender shrubs are put in there for protection. Hardwood can be allowed to bleach or be oiled to preserve the colour.

Ananas bracteatus is a bromeliad. There is a decorative, variegated form with narrow, drooping leaves. It is a native of Brazil. The variegated variety is *Ananas comosus* var. *variegatus*. For flowering it needs 20–27°C.

Agave can live for a hundred years, especially *A. americana* which is tall and broad. It is not suitable for a small greenhouse but it is impressive on a large stand as a focal point in a large, high conservatory or greenhouse. There are variegated forms.

Callistemon, bottle brush, takes its name from the flowers. They are bright red with yellow tips to the petals. The leaves are fine, and grey-green. The shrub will reach 4m (13ft); in the smaller greenhouse it needs pruning. Minimum temperature 4 –7°C.

If a conservatory does not suit the historical setting a light summer-house can be built like this one which provides winter storage for pots. It is a pleasant place to sit both in spring and autumn.

Following page: A courtyard can be planted in such a way that it is a pleasure to spend time there, even if other people use it as well.

Acknowledgments of photographs

A.J. van der Horst, Amsterdam: title page, pages 6 left, 7, 10, 11, 13 above, 14, 17, 20, 25 right, 26, 27 left, 28, 29, 30 left, 31, 33, 34, 35, 36 above, 38, 39, 40 left, 41, 42, 43, 45, 46, 47, 48, 49, 50, 51 right, 52 below, 53 right, 55, 57 left, 58 below, 60 right, 61, 62, 65, 67, 69, 71 below, 74, 75, 76, 78, 79, 80, 82 left, 83, 88, 90, 91, 92, 93, 95 below, 96, 97, 98, 99, 100, 101 right, 102 above, 103, 106, 109, 111 right, 113, 114, 115, 116, 119, 125 left, 126, 128, 129, 131, 132, 136, 137 below, 140, 141 right

M. Kurpershoek, Amsterdam: pages 16, 25 left, 27 right, 37, 40 right, 54, 60 left, 82 right, 85, 101 left, 102 below, 107, 111 left, 122, 130, 135, 141 left, 142, 143

G. Otter, Ijsselstein: pages 6 right, 18 below, 72 right, 104 below, 108, 110 above, 117, 123, 125 right, 133

P. Schut, Haarlem: pages 12, 15, 18 above, 19, 30 right, 44, 51 left, 52 above, 53 left, 56, 57 right, 58 above, 63, 64, 66, 68, 70, 71 above, 72, 73, 77, 81, 84, 87, 89, 94, 95 above, 104 above, 110 below, 118, 120, 121 below, 124, 127, 137 above, 138, 139

N. Vermeulen, Groningen: pages 9, 13 below, 36 below, 86, 121 above

The author would like to thank Rianne van Bergen, Amsterdam, for her invaluable help in the preparation of this book.